Getting to know me

© Louis Gill

First published 1999

Published by
Nash Pollock Publishing
32 Warwick Street
Oxford OX4 1SX

10 9 8 7 6 5 4 3 2 1

Orders to:
York Publishing Services
64 Hallfield Road
Layerthorpe
York YO3 7XQ

The author's moral right is asserted.

All rights reserved. No part of this publication may be reproduced, stored in a retrieval system, or transmitted in any form or by any means, electronic, mechanical, photocopying or otherwise, without the prior permission of Nash Pollock Publishing.

A catalogue record of this book is available from the British Library.

ISBN: 1 898255 28 8

Design and typesetting by Black Dog Design, Buckingham
Printed in Great Britain by T J International Ltd, Padstow

Getting to know me

A REFLECTIVE APPROACH TO ASSEMBLIES AND PSE

Louis Gill

Nash Pollock Publishing

Acknowledgements

The author and publishers gratefully acknowledge permission to publish the following extracts:

p 59: 'I had a little cat' by Charles Causley, from *All Day Saturday and Other Poems* (Macmillan)

p 74: 'Orders of the day' by John Cunliffe, from *A Second Poetry Book* (Oxford University Press)

p 87: 'Questions' by Eric Finney

p 90: 'It can't be done' by William J Bennett, from *The Children's Book of Virtues* (Simon and Schuster)

p 96: 'Talk to the animals' by Leslie Bricusse, © 1967 EMI Catalogue Partnership and EMI Hastings Catalog Inc., USA, reproduced by kind permission of IMP Ltd.

p 101: 'The seven commandments according to Mum' by Jacquelin Brown

p 139: 'The house at night' by James Kirkup

The publishers have made every effort to trace copyright holders and would be pleased to hear from those that have not been traced.

CONTENTS

Who Am I?	4
On a Desert Island	8
These are a Few of My Favourite Things	11
There's No-one Quite Like You	14
Going Places	17
Radiators and Drains	21
Body Language	24
What's in a Smile?	27
People Need People	30
Loneliness	33
Alone	36
Anger	39
Fear	43
Sadness	47
Happiness	51
Honesty	55
Trust	58
What Makes a Hero?	62
Caring For and Caring About	65
I Wish	69
Freedom	74
A Bit of Peace	79
Curiosity	84

The Amazing World of Mankind	88
The Wonderful World of Nature	92
Other Worlds	95
Rules and Commandments	99
Life is Not a Video Recorder!	104
Good Times and Bad Times	108
Is There Any Body There?	112
Touch	117
Thinking	121
Seeing	125
Noticing	131
Patterns	135
Silence and Sound	139
Labels and Stereotypes	144
What If?	148
Them and Us	152
Points of View	157

INTRODUCTION

What is *Getting to Know Me*?

Getting to Know Me is a collection of topic-based stimulus material designed to encourage pupils to reflect on who they are, what they stand for, how they relate to others, and how they relate to the world around them.

Schools are required by law to enable pupils 'to reflect on their experiences in a way which develops their spiritual awareness and self-knowledge'. The material will assist the process of 'making connections' and 'reflecting'. In relation to each topic, questions are asked which invite a personal response from pupils.

Who is it for?

Getting to Know Me is designed for use by teachers leading assemblies, and/or active tutorial or PSE programmes. It will be especially useful for class assemblies, where opportunities for follow-up activities are more readily available. The material has been written with the junior age range in mind but, with slight adaptation, it is equally well-suited to the lower secondary years.

The material

The choice of topics has been guided by three aims:
- to sharpen pupils' awareness of the world around them – the world of people, things and places;
- to increase their awareness of the world within them – their own feelings, responses and reactions;
- to help pupils use these and other experiences as they reflect upon who they are – what they stand for, their values, attitudes, beliefs and aspirations.

These aims can be represented in diagram form:

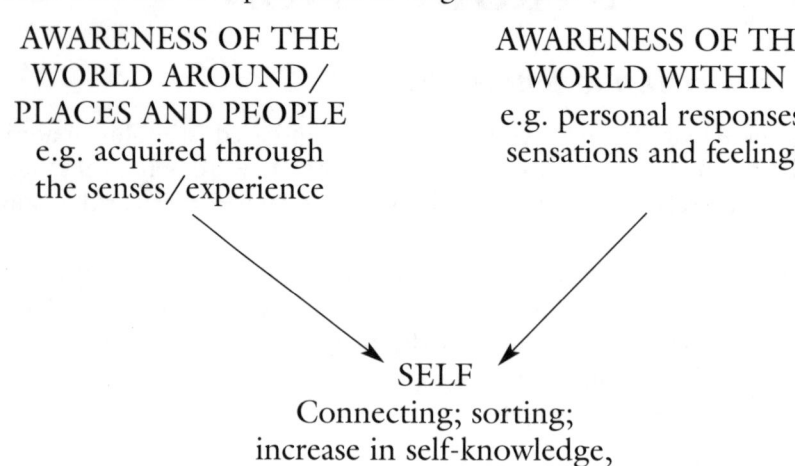

The material for each topic is arranged in four sections:

Focus: stating the aim(s) for the topic;

For reflection: the 'key' passage, which introduces the topic and provides a framework for reflection and associated ideas;

Things to do: follow-up activities which explore the theme further through creative tasks and discussion;

See also: a list of related topics.

How should it be used?

The *For reflection* passage is designed to be used either as part of an assembly, or as the introduction to a more extensive programme of work on the chosen theme.

In either case, the passage aims actively to involve pupils, and an essential feature of the material is the expectation that there will be a personal response to each question. The shape and unfolding of a topic assume that this process is taking place.

Sometimes the response will be a private one and, of course, a pupil's privacy must be respected. But often, personal responses can and should be shared with others, both to demonstrate differences in experience or opinion, and also to expand and develop a wider understanding of the topic under discussion. For this reason the material is better suited to use with class or year groups, rather than with the whole school.

Opportunities for thought and reflection have to be created. Thinking and reflecting are activities which require time – they need 'breathing space' and, often, they benefit from a few moments silence.

Where a *For reflection* passage is used in an assembly, it is important to plan also for what will happen next, after the time for reflection. Too often the impact of a thought-provoking assembly is lost because of the untimely introduction of an activity in contrasting mood, such as the celebrating of pupils' achievements or the reprimanding of inappropriate behaviour.

The length of a 'pause for thought' will depend upon the particular activity and individual circumstances. If a pause is too long, there will be a loss of pace, probably accompanied by a loss of interest. If the pause is too short, questions requiring a carefully considered response will, instead, become rhetorical and the level of pupil participation will be reduced. It is important for teachers to be sufficiently familiar with the material to determine where pauses are needed and for how long they should be sustained. A frequent sharing of responses assists both pace and interest levels.

For teachers wishing to use the material as part of an active tutorial or personal and social education programme, the *Things to do* section for each topic suggests an appropriate range of follow-up activities. The 'creative' nature of many of the tasks will require pupils to explore their responses from different perspectives. The activities provide opportunities for pupils to work as individuals, in pairs or in small groups, as well as in whole class or larger groups. While the quality of pupils' work will obviously be acknowledged and valued, it is important to remember at all times that the focus should be constantly on process – on raising pupils' awareness, and on encouraging them to question how and why they are making particular decisions and choices.

It is hoped *Getting to Know Me* will provide a stimulus leading to further thoughts and reflections. It is expected that teachers may wish to add or substitute alternative personal or topical examples. Please use the ideas and material flexibly and imaginatively.

WHO AM I?

Focus

To encourage self-awareness and self-knowledge by comparing how we see ourselves with how others see us.

For reflection

Have you ever walked through a hall of mirrors – the sort you often find at seaside resorts or at fairgrounds?

In a hall of mirrors each mirror distorts or changes your appearance in some way. Through one mirror you can appear very short and very fat; through another, very tall and very thin. In a third, your face is made to look like that of a frightening monster, while in a fourth you have great, long hairpin legs, with a tiny body perched on top. And so it goes on. Each mirror changes your appearance so much that, at the end, you are left wondering, 'Who am I? What do I really look like?'

Something similar might happen if different people were asked to describe what you are like – not what you *look* like, but *the sort of person you are.*

For example:

If someone asked your mother to describe you, what do you think she would say? She might describe you as caring, happy, helpful, untidy, lazy – there are many, many words she could choose. But remember, mothers are usually very honest and will include both good points and weaknesses! So, think for a moment, how do you think she would describe you?

How might your class teacher describe you?

Would different teachers describe you differently? Why is that?

How might your best friend describe you?

Of these different descriptions, which do you think would be most accurate?

Who is right?

What are you *really* like? Who are you?

How would *you* describe yourself? Be honest!

What are your strongest *personal qualities* – not your skills and abilities, your personal qualities?

What are your weakest points?

So that's how you see yourself.

Now, one last question: how would you describe the sort of person you would really *like to be*?

Remember, you are not being asked about your appearance, nor about whether you would like to be rich and famous. The question is *what sort of person* would you really like to be?

If the person you would like to be is different from the person you are, how can you become that new person – what changes do you need to make?

What are you going to *do* about it?

Things to do

1 As with all evaluation tasks, it is important that the assessments and comments pupils wish to make are not constrained by the limits of their linguistic and literary skills. It is as important for a pupil with learning difficulties to participate fully in activities as it is for his or her classmates. The following list of words/descriptors (or some similar selection) could be discussed with pupils and used as a prompt for responses to the six key questions identified in the main text. Alternatively, a list could be compiled as a whole class/group activity.

smart	generous	lacks concentration
noisy/talkative	untidy	lazy
caring	tries hard/perseveres	quiet
prefers to work alone	careless	helpful
selfish	can be trusted	aggressive/short tempered
conscientious	happy/cheerful	reliable
needs to be supervised	cautious	enjoys group work
friendly	serious	curious/questioning
adventurous	boisterous	shy

6 Getting to know me

It is important for pupils to discuss *why* others see us differently from how we see ourselves, and *why* their opinions differ from each other.

2 Suggest that, using a mirror in the privacy of their own homes, pupils should discuss with their image what they have learned about themselves, and should consider whether they need to make changes – whether they need to improve themselves in particular ways.

A discussion of the following poem could provide a starting point:

The Mirror

I looked into a mirror
To see what I could see
But the image that I saw there
Did not belong to me.

At least I did not think so
Until I paused to find
That the picture I expected
Was only in my mind.

Donald McMillan (aged 11)

3 Ask pupils to write a paragraph, for use on the Internet, in which they introduce themselves to a complete stranger. Pupils should first consider the questions they would want answered if they were the stranger. The description should be interesting and informative and should leave the stranger with the feeling that he or she knows the writer, even though they have never met.

4 Creating self-portraits in sound: invite each pupil to select any classroom percussion instrument, the sound of which, they feel, matches their personality. Using the chosen instrument, the task will be to create a short piece (ten seconds is sufficient) which expresses the sort of person they are.

Points for pupils to consider include:
timbre – the type/quality of sound the instrument makes;
pitch – high or low sound;
manner of performance – whether it will be appropriate to play the instrument brusquely or gently;

rhythm – lively or relaxed;
dynamics – loud or soft: maybe, contrasting;
tempo – fast or slow.

It may be effective for a phrase or figure to be repeated more than once. The individual self-portraits should be recorded and linked to form a class/group 'photograph'.

(See also 'There's No-one Quite Like You' *Things to do*. If the 'personal designs' are photographed using slide film, the visual images and the recorded music self-portraits can be combined to provide an audio/visual presentation.)

See also

These are a Few of My Favourite Things

There's No-one Quite Like You

Going Places

Points of View

Radiators and Drains

ON A DESERT ISLAND

Focus

To encourage pupils to recognise, reflect upon and appreciate people and things that make a significant contribution to the quality of their lives.

For reflection

How would you like to be shipwrecked on a desert island? Just imagine it: lots of sun, lots of sand, lots of sea and no school! It sounds like heaven, doesn't it, until you realise that you are alone on the island. There is no television and no radio; no supermarket from which to buy food; no-one to make meals, and no shelter unless you make something yourself. If you want to eat, you will have to gather together your own food, either from plants growing in the wild, or by hunting and fishing with equipment made from whatever bits and pieces you can find.

In the radio programme *Desert Island Discs,* famous celebrities are asked to imagine that they have been shipwrecked on a desert island. There is no-one else on the island. In this imaginary situation they are allowed to have with them eight records, one book and one luxury item – and the luxury item must not be a means of escape from the island (such as an inflatable dinghy), nor a form of radio communication (such as a radio or telephone).

If you were the celebrity guest on the programme, which records would you choose? How would you make your choice? For example, would you choose recordings that reminded you of particular people, or particular occasions?

Which book would you select?

And which luxury item – perhaps a favourite game or toy, or something that is very important to you?

Now imagine, for a moment, that *you really are alone on a desert island.*

Who are the *people* you miss most?

What *things* do you miss?

What *sights, sounds, smells and tastes* do you miss?

Isn't it true that the most important people and the most important things in our lives – those we would find it difficult to manage without –

are often the ones we take for granted and fail to appreciate until they're not there for us? But it doesn't *have* to be that way! And we shouldn't need to be cast away on a desert island before we can realise who and what things matter most to us. What can we do and say to show how much we value the *people* who do so much for us? How can we say 'thank you' in deeds as well as words?

Things to do

1 Making a personal selection of records and items to take to the desert island should be undertaken as an individual activity. It doesn't matter in the slightest if pupils cannot produce a complete list. The process – thinking about *why* they are making the choice – is more important than the outcome.

   Of course, the results can be used in a variety of ways (e.g. group/whole class discussion, wall display etc.) but take care to ensure that the purpose of the activity is made clear at all times.

2 When pupils are identifying the people they would miss most, encourage them to think about the quality and nature of their relationships by stating *why* a particular person is important to them, and ask sensitively for a practical example of that relationship.
   Pupils might also find it helpful to break the activity down to consider

   loved ones

   close friends

   others.

3 The private diary: encourage pupils to keep a *private* diary for an agreed period, say a week. Each day they are to record, very briefly, any occasions or situations when people, things or happenings affect their lives.

   For example, pupils might note
   - instances of contact with others – things done *for* the pupils, and things done *by* the pupils to help others;
   - their feelings and reactions to things or situations they especially enjoy or dislike;
   - things they observe;
   - new experiences etc.

The purpose of this task is to raise pupils' awareness of their dependence upon, and interaction with, the world around them. Pupils may or may not wish to share their experiences with others. It is a private diary and their privacy should be respected, unless they choose otherwise.

4 Help pupils to brainstorm different ways of showing appreciation – of saying thank you.

See also

These are a Few of My Favourite Things

People Need People

Alone

THESE ARE A FEW OF MY FAVOURITE THINGS

Focus

To show that the things we choose to have around us, and the experiences we value, are expressions of the sort of people we are.

For reflection

What are your favourite things?

What are the things that give you most pleasure?

Are there foods you really, really like?

Are there things you especially like doing after school and at weekends?

Do you have a favourite game or toy, or a bicycle or a skateboard?

Do you have a pet?

Do you have a favourite book or books?

What music do you like?

What are your favourite television programmes?

Are there friends you enjoy being with – friends who make you laugh?

Are there people who make you feel good because they understand you and you can rely on them?

Are there places you particularly enjoy visiting?

Is there a place in your home where you feel cosy and comfortable – a place you think of as being 'yours'?

Are there special times you like to remember because you enjoyed them so much?

The things we like, and the things we don't like, provide important clues to help us discover more about ourselves. The friends we choose, and how we use our time, provide further clues.

Think carefully about the answers you have given, and you might learn quite a good deal about yourself. To find out what the clues tell you will require a little detective work.

You have probably seen the television programme *Through the Keyhole* in which three celebrities in the studio are shown a short video of rooms inside the house of a famous person. They look for clues to try to decide how old the famous person is, whether they are male or female, what interests they have etc. And then the panel is asked, 'Who would live in a house like this?' If they have been observant, and if they have asked the right questions, the celebrities are often able to guess the name of the person who lives in the house.

Imagine the camera crew visited your bedroom when you were not in. Because you're not famous – yet! – the question would need to be changed slightly to ask, not 'Who?' but '*What sort of person* would live in a room like this?'

From the clues available to them, what answers do you think the panel of celebrities might give? Do you think their answers would agree with the sort of person *you* think you are?

Things to do

1 The opening of the extract invites individual responses to a series of questions, the answers to which provide each pupil with a personal profile. Whether the questions are presented to a large group, smaller groups, or to individuals, sufficient time should be allowed for pupils to make a considered response. Pupils should always be encouraged to reflect on *why* they make the choices they do.

2 '*Through the Keyhole*': as amateur detectives investigating the room of a stranger, what clues would pupils look for to help them decide the sort of person who lives there?
   - Applying the same criteria and questions to their own bedroom or to the responses given to the earlier questions, what do the pupils learn about themselves?
   - If pupils knew that their rooms were to be searched, what five items would each leave around as examples of their interests and personality?

3 In the song song, 'These are a Few of My Favourite Things' from *The Sound of Music*, Maria lists things to do with the senses and simple, enjoyable experiences. She does not include expensive possessions. For example, she chooses things associated with
sight: 'raindrops on roses'; 'cream coloured ponies'; 'wild geese that

fly with the moon on their wings'; 'girls in white dresses with blue satin sashes'; 'silver white winters'
sound: doorbells and sleighbells'
touch: 'whiskers on kittens'; 'warm woollen mittens'; 'snowflakes that stay on my nose and eyelashes'
taste and smell: 'crisp apple strudels'; 'schnizel with noodles'
moments of excitement: 'brown paper packages tied up with strings'.

Ask pupils to close their eyes and imagine that they are experiencing the feelings, sights and sensations described, as you slowly read to them these descriptions from the song.

This list is a very personal one, belonging only to Maria. Ask pupils to produce their own persoanl lists of favourite sensuous experiences.

The effectiveness of this activity will be enhanced if a recording of 'These are a Few of my Favourite Things' is used as a stimulus resource.

4 Working either individuaaly or in small groups, and using the song as a model, create alternative lyrics.

Before they begin, ask pupils to close their eyes and imagine that they are experiencing the feelings, sights and sensations described, as you read to them the words of the song.

Draw attention to the fact that all of Maria's favourite things have to do with the senses and with enjoyable experiences, and not with possessions.

See also

On a Desert Island

There's No-one Quite Like You

Who Am I?

Going Places

THERE'S NO-ONE QUITE LIKE YOU

Focus

To encourage each pupil to recognise, respect and value his or her uniqueness.

For reflection

Do you realise that there's no-one else quite like you? Just think for a moment. Is there anyone else who looks exactly like you? Is there anyone else who has the same colour eyes, and the same shaped nose and eyebrows, and is the same size and body shape?

Is there anyone with the same fingerprints?

Do you know that scientists are able to identify a person by examining just a single hair, and police scientists often identify a dead body by checking dental records?

But you are also different from everyone else by being *who* you are, besides being different in appearance. For example:

What sort of person are you?

Are you shy? Are you confident?

Do you like to spend time alone? Do you prefer to be with friends?

Are you quiet? Are you talkative?

Are you a bit of a joker? Are you serious?

Are you lazy? Are you hardworking?

Are you patient? Do you persevere with a problem?

Are you impatient? Do you give up easily?

Do you like to ask questions to find out how and why things are as they are?

Are you a helpful sort of person?

What do you really enjoy doing? Do you enjoy making things? Do you enjoy taking things to pieces to discover how they work? Do you enjoy reading (what sort of books do you enjoy)? Do you enjoy painting pictures, or playing an instrument, or singing? Do you like sport – do you like playing games? Do you like being in the countryside? Do you like collecting flowers? Do you enjoy doing sums or performing experiments? Which are your favourite television programmes?

What are you good at – not just in school, but generally? What are you not very good at?

Do you say what you think, or do you wait to hear what others say?

Can you make *choices* for yourself, or do you depend on others?

Your answers to these questions are unlikely to be exactly the same as those of anyone else. There is no-one else like you. You are *unique* – and that obviously makes you a special person.

Respect the fact that you are unique. Think for yourself. Make up your own mind. *Don't be afraid of being different – but don't be different just for the sake of being different.*

Things to do

1 *Physical appearance.* A simple activity is to choose a group of pupils of the same height, and then invite other pupils to identify any similarities or distinguishing differences e.g. colour of eyes; shape of nose, mouth, chin, ears; size of hands, feet, waist(?) etc. What are the significant distinguishing features?

2 *What sort of person are you?* The list of descriptions provided can obviously be added to or, even, replaced. Whatever list is used, it will be helpful if the activity is structured to accommodate both self-assessment and the views of others.

3 *What do you really enjoy doing?* Pupils should prepare a personal response to each of the questions asked and then compare their responses with others, through pair or small group work, to identify similarities as well as differences.

4 *What are you good at?* The question should be interpreted as widely as possible, and should certainly not be confined to school subjects. For example, some pupils are good listeners, some display patience and caring qualities, others perform well in out of school activities. Often pupils are not good at recognising their own strengths, especially if they have learning difficulties, and positive comments from others should be welcomed.

5 Encourage pupils to examine how independent they are in the views they express and the choices they make. How and when might they be influenced by others? How can they distinguish bad influences from good?

6 Provide each pupil with a piece of paper (A5 size will do) on which he/she is asked to draw any continuous-lined shape (i.e. the beginning and end of the line meet without taking the pencil off the paper) which they feel expresses the sort of person they are. It can be any shape – smooth (e.g. like an amoeba) or jagged (e.g. like a star), geometric or irregular, using straight or curved lines etc. Whatever shape the pupil feels best represents him or her.

Then invite pupils to fill in the shape using their favourite colour. Allow colour mixes if necessary.

The 'personal designs' will no doubt encourage discussion and comment.(See also 'Who am I?' *Things to do* 'Creating self-portraits in sound')

See also

Who Am I?

These are a Few of My Favourite Things

On a Desert Island

Labels and Stereotypes

GOING PLACES

Focus

To help pupils learn more about themselves by looking closely at how they relate to places – their likes and dislikes.

For reflection

If you were the winner of a quiz programme on TV, and the prize was a free air ticket to anywhere in the world, where would you choose to go? Why would you want to go there? What is it about the place that appeals to you?

If you were offered a trip to the moon, would you go?

Or would you prefer to stay at home?

Places are important to us for different reasons:

> Home is the place where we are cared for and where we have our own belongings around us;
>
> School is … well, how would you describe school? Do you like school? How important is it in your life?
>
> There are other places we like to go to, such as a friend's house or the home of a favourite relative, where we know we will enjoy ourselves.
>
> And we sometimes have a 'den' – somewhere that is special.
>
> Then there may be places we would like to visit just to to find out what they're like.

The fact is, when we speak about places, we all have different likes and dislikes. Some people like to visit hot countries: others can't stand the heat and prefer somewhere cool. Some like to live in large cities or towns, while others much prefer to live in small villages. Some would like to live in a castle: others would prefer to live in a small cottage with a thatched roof. When we each look at our own likes and dislikes, the sort of people we are gradually becomes clear.

Think, for a few moments, of your favourite places – and think *why* you enjoy them.

Then think of the places, or the sort of places, you definitely don't like – and think *why* you dislike them so.

Do you have a favourite holiday place?

Do you prefer to be in the town or in the countryside?

Do you like to visit a place by yourself (or perhaps with a special friend) or do you like to be part of a crowd?

Where do you choose to go in your free time (for example, do you like going to a park or playground, to a football stadium, to a swimming pool, to a cinema, to the library, to the fairground, or is there somewhere else you prefer)?

Do you enjoy the outdoor life – camping, hiking, and making your own food?

Have you ever been to a theme park – perhaps Disneyworld?

Have you enjoyed visiting a place of historic interest - a place that helps us to understand something of life in the past (such as the city of York, or the ruins of a castle, or any other important building, for example)?

Is there any one place that, above all others, is very special to you?

Now think back over the answers you have given. There are no right or wrong answers. But what sort of person do they describe? Do they describe someone who is outward-going and enjoys being with lots of other people in places where there is plenty of entertainment; someone who is adventurous and likes to visit unusual places; someone who is independent and doesn't particularly enjoy crowds; someone who enjoys visiting places to learn something new ... or someone who is a mixture?

We often learn most about ourselves (the sort of people we are) when we look closely at how we relate to things, places and people – our likes and dislikes.

When you have thought about your own answers, you may like to find out what answers a friend gave, and decide whether those answers match the type of person you know him or her to be.

Things to do

General comment
During work on this topic pupils should constantly be required to explain *why* they are making a particular decision. Often a second 'Why?' will cause the pupil to reflect more deeply on his or her response.

1 In several instances, the passage requires pupils to make a straight choice between two alternatives, even though that choice will be guided by the responses to the persistent 'Why?' question.

It will be possible for pupils to collate the answers and present the information in chart form as a piece of market research – a whole class/group profile (e.g. how many preferred …?)

It may be that the individual choices of some pupils will match the group profile. However, as the reponses to other questions are added, the unique character of each individual's profile is likely to become increasingly apparent – especially if reasons behind the choices are taken into consideration.

2 Divide the class/group into small groups of five or six. Appoint one pupil in each group as a regional TV reporter.

Imagine that it is the middle of the week prior to a bank holiday weekend. The reporter interviews each group member to ask how he or she will *ideally* be spending the coming weekend. The interviewer's questions should include:

> Why the group member plans to spend the weekend in the chosen manner;
>
> What he or she expects to do;
>
> Who else will be involved, etc.

An extension of this activity might be to appoint one pupil as a national TV producer, who then selects a group of interesting and contrasting responses to form a national news item.

To increase authenticity the interviews can be recorded using either an audio or video recorder.

An alternative activity might be to use the material for a newspaper article.

3 '*A special place of my own*': Working first in small groups, ask pupils to share with others where they 'retreat' to when they wish to be alone. What is special about this place? Is it purely private, or is it sometimes used by others?

4 Ask pupils to write a letter to a pen friend in which they describe one of their favourite places. They should say what is so special about the

place they choose, and try to describe why they feel the way they do about it. The place can be where they live, somewhere they have visited or, maybe, somewhere they would really like to visit.

See also

These are a Few of My Favourite Things

There's No-one Quite Like You

Who Am I?

RADIATORS AND DRAINS

Focus

To help pupils appreciate the effect they have on others by their general attitude, by their behaviour, and by the moods they display.

For reflection

Do people smile when you come into a room and look pleased to see you? Or do you think they're pleased to see the back of you when you leave? All of us have an effect on other people by the way we behave and by our attitude to life. And, of course, other people have an effect on us. There are some people we enjoy being with and there are others we find a bit of a drag. We might call the first group 'radiators' and the second group 'drains'!

Here are descriptions of the two types. Listen carefully to decide which group you belong to.

A *'radiator'* person

- is fun to be with, is always cheerful and sees the bright side of life;
- is lively and can often suggest fun things to do;
- can see the good in other people rather than the bad;
- is optimistic and believes that things will work out for the best;
- is sympathetic and understanding – listens carefully to your problems and helps you to find a way of overcoming them;
- appreciates anything that other people do for him or her by saying 'thank you' and by doing something in return at some other time;
- shows appreciation for a present – even if all of his or her friends have bought the same thing!
- tries to agree with what you say;
- will always congratulate you when you do something well, and will say complimentary things to you.

A 'radiator' person *leaves you feeling better* for having been in their company.

A *'drain'* person

- is always moaning and complaining – and often says 'It's all right for you!'
- is often bored and can't find anything to do;

- sees faults in other people rather than noticing their good points;
- is pessimistic and believes that things will never get better;
- is not sympathetic and understanding – is only interested in his or her own problems and, whatever you say, can always think of something worse that has happened to them;
- does not thank people for things they have done – thinks they shouldn't need thanking;
- when given a present, will let you know by word or by the expression on their face, that this is not what they wanted and you should have bought something else;
- always seems to find fault with the things you say;
- is often jealous of someone else's success and says, 'Well, of course, I could have done better than you if I'd wanted to';

A 'drain' person leaves you thinking *'Thank goodness he's gone!'*

Are you a 'radiator' or a 'drain'? What effect do you have on people?

What qualities do you have that other people like and enjoy?

Do you have any qualities or habits that other people don't much like and, perhaps, find irritating?

Do you need to change in any way?

Things to do

1 Divide pupils into small groups of five or six. Each group is identified (for this exercise) either as a 'radiator' group or as a 'drain' group.

   The pupils in each group will then organise themselves as if in preparation for a group photograph, and each pupil within a group will invent something to say which is in keeping with the label the group has been given (i.e. pupils in the 'radiator' groups will think of comments which are positive, optimistic or cheerful, while pupils in the 'drain' groups will express negative, pessimistic or miserable thoughts). Pupils should also prepare appropriate facial expressions, postures and gestures to match what they have to say.

   At the instruction 'freeze', all action is frozen as if for the photograph, but the identity of the groups should be apparent from the facial expressions and postures.

When a pupil is tapped on the shoulder by you, he or she will come temporarily to life, deliver their prepared comment, acting in role, and then become frozen once more.

The task enables pupils (a) to experience the particular emotion, (b) to experience the reactions of others to that emotion, and (c) to observe body language. (See also 'Body Language'.)

It is helpful for the identity labels of the groups to be exchanged so that pupils have the opportunity to compare their experience of the contrasting emotions.

2 Is it possible to change a 'drain' person into a 'radiator'?

Ask pupils, working in small groups, to list as many ways as they can think of for changing the attitudes of people who regularly express negative thoughts and behave in a depressing manner. (Perhaps a 'swear' box?!)

Is it possible to change 'nuisance' pupils into useful members of the class? How?

3 Using suitable images cut out from colour supplements and magazines, construct two class/group collages, a 'radiator' collage and a 'drain' collage. Invite pupils to suggest a range of suitable captions or comments for enclosing in thought balloons.

4 Using either card or papier-mâché, pupils should design and make 'radiator' and 'drain' masks.

Encourage pupils to experiment with the masks to discover
- how people react to the contrasting expressions;
- whether wearing the mask naturally suggests a type of behaviour;
- what happens when the mask worn suggests one emotion but the words spoken represent a contrasting mood.

See also

What's in a Smile?

Body Language.

Who Am I?

BODY LANGUAGE

Focus

To raise pupils' awareness of body language as an integral (and, sometimes, involuntary) part of inter-personal communication.

For reflection

Have you ever watched television with the sound switched off?

Often – just by watching people's faces and the movement of their eyes, and by watching the way they use their hands and the way they move – we can get a good idea of what is taking place, even though we can't hear what is being said.

In a similar way we can watch a group of pupils in the playground, or the crowd at a football match, or shoppers talking at a bus stop, or demonstrators on a protest march, or people sitting in a dentist's waiting room. In each case, there could be signals in the way the people behave that provide clues to what they are feeling. We don't always need to hear the words to get the message.

'Actions speak louder than words', people say. In fact we use the expression *body language* to describe how people's movements and actions tell us what they are inwardly thinking or feeling. We all use body language and often we don't realise the signals we are sending out.

Let us try an experiment.

Using only your right hand and no words, how would you

- greet a friend?
- ask for something?
- call someone?
- threaten someone?
- tell someone to calm down?
- ask someone to make less noise?

By watching a person's hands, how might you tell if that person is nervous about something?

Using only your eyes, and without moving the rest of your face, how can you

- look sad?
- look suspicious?
- look angry?
- look cheeky?
- look bored?

By watching a person's eyes, how might you tell if that person is not telling the truth?

Using your shoulders, how can you

– look confident?   – look as if you couldn't care less?

Of course, not all movements are as obvious as these, but it helps when someone is speaking to us if we *watch* what their body is telling us while *listening* to what they say. Sometimes a person's body language tells us more than the words they are speaking, especially if they are very pleased, excited, sad or afraid. When we look for the signs, as well as listen to the words, the message becomes much clearer.

One last point: whether you are speaking to someone, or listening to what they have to say, think what body language messages *you* are sending out.

Sometimes actions really do speak louder than words!

Things to do

1 Divide the class/group into pairs and give each pair two or three 'thoughts' from the list below. Ask pupils to rehearse gestures and facial expressions (i.e. mime only) that will communicate their thoughts to someone else, or to an audience:
   a 'Please be quiet! I'm trying to read!'
   b 'Go away! You're annoying me!'
   c 'Now, which one of you is next?'
   d 'Have you heard the news?'
   e 'Honestly, I didn't do it,'
   f 'I think it's round the corner.'
   g 'Look what I've found!'
   h 'Please can you reach that box on the top shelf for me?'

   The thoughts can then be performed to the rest of the class/group in three ways:
   - Using only gestures to convey the meaning (i.e. no words);
   - Using words only (for this interpretation those in the 'audience' should either be blindfolded, or close their eyes);
   - Using words and actions simultaneously.

   What differences do pupils experience?

2 *'Statues'*: Working individually, pupils remain in one place, with both feet on the ground, but moving their face and limbs through a range of expressions and dramatic gestures until they are instructed to 'freeze'. They must then hold their position and facial expression.

When invited by the teacher, a pupil will 'come alive' and will suggest a thought which matches the frozen position. Unless spoken to by the teacher, all pupils remain silent in their frozen positions.

This activity is the reverse of the previous one, which led from the thought to the action.

3 Through the use of voice inflection and body language, ask pupils to interpret the expression 'Oh!' in fifteen different ways.

4 Construct a class/group collage comprising body language images cut from colour supplements, magazines and newspapers. The finished piece should illustrate as wide a range of expressions and emotions as possible, and should include subtle as well as dramatic gestures and facial expressions.

A supplementary activity could require pupils to add 'thought balloons', or to suggest appropriate captions.

See also

Is There Any Body There?

What's in a Smile?

Radiators and Drains

WHAT'S IN A SMILE?

Focus

To value the importance of a smile in everyday relationships.

For reflection

What is a smile?

How can we tell when someone is smiling? What does it look like? What happens to the eyes, the mouth, the cheeks, the eyebrows?

What is the difference between a smile and a laugh?

Do smiles come in different shapes and sizes? Well, let's find out. Let's all smile now and notice the differences between our expressions. Remember, we're smiling not laughing!

What sort of feelings make us want to smile?

There are two main causes why we smile. The first is *when things happen* or when we remember things that have already happened – things that amuse us, or give us a feeling of pleasure or satisfaction.

Can you recall things that have happened that made you smile – things that amused you at the time, or pleased you, or gave you a feeling of satisfaction?

The second cause for smiling is *as a signal* to another person or persons. It is a signal which says 'Let's be friends'. If, for example, you meet someone who smiles at you, the natural reaction is to smile back in return. There is an understanding between you that you are not enemies. If, on the other hand, you meet someone who scowls at you, what is your reaction?

We use a smile as a sign of friendship many times during the course of each day. Even our pets understand smiles. When we smile the family dog wags its tail and there is a twinkle in its eye.

Using a smile is like putting oil on a bicycle chain – it makes everything work more smoothly. For example, can you recall occasions when, perhaps, you have done something wrong and you have sheepishly smiled at mum or dad or the teacher, in the hope that they will forgive you?

We also use a smile as a signal when we want to cheer someone up, or when we are showing sympathy because they have been disappointed or hurt in some way.

The value of a smile is well described in this poem, by an unknown poet. It iis called, quite simply, 'A Smile'.

A Smile

A smile costs nothing and yet produces a lot.
It enriches he who receives it
Without making he who gives it any the poorer.
It only lasts an instant
But the memory it leaves sometimes lasts forever.
No one is rich enough to be able to do without one;
No one is so poor he does not merit one.
It creates happiness in the home.
It is a tangible sign of friendship.
A smile makes he who is tired feel rested,
Gives new heart to those who are down.
It cannot be bought, nor loaned, nor stolen,
For it is a thing which has value
Only the moment it is given.
And if, from time to time, you should meet someone
Who no longer knows how to smile,
Be generous – give him yours,
For no one quite needs a smile as much
As he who cannot give one to others.

Isn't life happier for everyone when people smile?

Even tasks we don't like doing – such as tidying-up and putting things away seem easier and less unpleasant when we smile. *We* feel better, and *others* feel better when *we* smile.

As the poet says
'A smile costs nothing and yet produces a lot'.

Just try it and see!

Things to do

1 The passage asks, 'Do smiles come in different shapes and sizes?'

   Ask pupils to use an appropriate smile for each of the following thoughts:
   a 'I know something you don't know!'
   b 'Isn't that beautiful?'

c 'Did you hear that? I've won!'
d 'Now Lisa, you will just feel a tiny prick. It won't hurt.'
e 'I don't really think you're funny, but I'd better smile!'
f 'Not today, thank you.'
g 'And then, what do you think happened?'
h 'Mmm. That was delicious!'
i 'I'm smarter than you.'
j 'I'm not sure I should trust you.'

2 Working in pairs, ask pupils to improvise short scenes in which the above comments or thoughts might have occurred.

3 *Either* ask pupils to collect images of people smiling. The images can be collected from any source e.g. newspapers, photographs, paintings, pictures of sculptures.

Or a selection can be provided by the teacher.

In either case the selection should cover as wide a range of situations as possible and should include the enigmatic as well as the obvious.

Pupils should then suggest suitable captions to explain the images, and alternative interpretations should be discussed.

4 *A 'smile' poem*: Ask pupils to individually produce simple statements of situations or happenings that make them smile. Each statement should begin:

'I smile ... (when) ... (if) ... (at) ... '

As previously, efforts should be made to obtain as wide a range of responses as possible. The statements should then be structured to form a class/group poem.

5 *'Smiles awareness day'*: To increase pupils' awareness of how frequently smiles play a part in everyday communication, organise a 'smiles awareness day', on which pupils note 'smile incidents', involving either themselves or others. Their observations should include the effect of the smile as well as the fact that it occurred.

6 See 'Radiators and Drains' *Things to do* 'mask' activity

See also
Body Language

Radiators and Drains

Happiness

PEOPLE NEED PEOPLE

Focus

To raise pupils' awareness of our dependence on other people – and their dependence on us.

For reflection

We need people! We need all sorts of people. For example, we need:

- Farmers and food producers – to make sure that we have plenty to eat;
- People who make things for us, and repair them when they're broken;
- People who bring things to us – such as postmen and milkmen; and people who take things away – such as the men who collect our rubbish;
- Doctors – to make us well when we are ill;
- Entertainers – to amuse us and make us laugh;
- People who take us where we want to go – such as bus or taxi drivers;
- People who sell things to us in shops.

These are all people who make or do things that we are able to use when we want to. They are people we know are there – we depend on them being there – and we can't easily manage without them.

Can you think of others who might be added to this list?

But we also depend on another group of people – the people who are around us every day: parents, brothers and sisters, teachers, friends; maybe even people we don't know particularly well, but who say or do something when we need help. These people provide the sort of things money can't buy – however rich we might be. We rely on them for love, for support, for ideas, for advice, for playing with, for arguing with, for sharing secrets with, for turning to when we have a problem that is worrying us, for giving presents to or receiving presents from. We need these people. Without them we would be very lonely.

Take yesterday, for example. Think of the people who played a part in your life. People who had made things you enjoyed using: people who took you where you wanted to go. People who provided things for you, or explained things to you. Think of those you talked with and played with.

Can you remember anyone who said or did doing something that pleased you?

Can you remember anyone who helped you in some way, however small?

We need people. But *people also need us* – for all the reasons we have said. Like us, they want to be loved and liked; they want someone to listen to them; they want support and advice; they want someone to play with, and so on. Above all they need people around them who make them feel good about themselves, who make them feel cheerful – who make them feel that *someone is interested in them*.

As you think back over yesterday, can you think of anything you said or did that helped someone else – perhaps something that brightened their day? Were there any occasions when you *might* have said or done something which would have been helpful, but you missed the opportunity? *We need people* but, remember, *they also need us!*

Things to do

1 Pupils should keep a diary for one day (obviously the period can be extended for enthusiastic pupils!) in which they record, however briefly, the contacts they have with other people, including family. In particular they should note the *nature* of the contact. For example, was it fun, was it helpful, was it supportive of the pupil? Or was it not very pleasant, perhaps annoying, boring or critical?

   Did anyone say or do anything that was helpful or encouraging?

   What did the pupil say or do that was helpful or encouraging to other people?

   If the day had comprised only *three* of those contacts, which would the pupil have wished those three to be?

2 Working individually, pupils should be asked to draw two diagrams. Central to each is the word 'ME', perhaps enclosed in a circle or rectangle.

   In the first diagram the pupil should encircle the word 'ME' with the names of those people upon whom he/she really depends on a daily basis. (The list should comprise only *contacts* i.e. it should exclude manufacturers, and people who provide services). From each name an arrow should be targeted at the word 'ME'.

In the second diagram the central 'ME' should be encircled with the names of those who are helped, or whose lives are made happier, by regular contact with the pupil. Arrows should radiate out from the word 'ME' to the names in the circle.

3 Divide pupils into groups of three or four. Ask the pupils in each group to discuss and list the qualities they would expect to find in a good friend. From the small group lists, collate and discuss a whole class/group list. Are any of the qualities considered to be more important than others?

Invite pupils to reflect privately on their own strengths and weaknesses as friends.

See also

Trust

On a Desert Island

Loneliness

Radiators and Drains

LONELINESS

Focus

To define loneliness (especially loneliness in childhood) as distinct from being alone;

To suggest ways of overcoming loneliness.

For reflection

Have you ever felt lonely – that is, have you ever felt unhappy because you seemed to have no friends?

Sometimes people make the mistake of thinking that being alone and being lonely mean the same thing, but that is not so.

Many people live *alone* but have good friends with whom they can enjoy themselves, and with whom they can discuss their problems or share their secrets. They may live alone, but they are certainly not lonely.

People who are *lonely* feel unhappy because they don't have close friends with whom to have fun, and with whom they can chat about things that are troubling them. They sometimes feel they have no-one who understands them.

You don't have to be alone to be lonely. You can live in a big city where there are thousands and thousands of people and still feel lonely, because there is no-one you can talk to who seems to really understand you.

Often loneliness is thought of as being associated with old age, and it is certainly true that an old person whose husband or wife has died can feel very lonely. After all, they have lost a close friend – someone with whom they have shared a great deal over many years.

But loneliness has nothing to do with age, and someone of any age, however young or old, can feel lonely. The main difference is that when you are young, loneliness doesn't often last long at any one time. For old people, loneliness can last many years.

So, now we are clear what is meant by being lonely, let us ask the question again:

Have you ever felt lonely?

The sorts of things that sometimes make pupils of your age feel lonely are:

- When you're the odd one out – when everyone else seems to be enjoying themselves, and no-one is interested in you;
- When you've not been invited to a party, and all your so-called friends are going;
- If you move to a new school and everyone else seems to be with groups of friends;
- When your best friend goes off with someone else;
- When you're the only one who can't do something, and no-one seems to care;
- If you have something that is worrying you and you don't know who to tell;
- If you are being bullied.

Have any of these things happened to you? Have there been other occasions when you have felt lonely?

How did the feeling of loneliness end? What changed? Was it something you did or said? Or, was it something someone else did or said?

The unhappiness caused by being lonely is something we all want to avoid, but if you become lonely, there are things you can do:
- Don't just feel sorry for yourself – that will make things worse rather than better;
- If the loneliness is likely to last only for a short time – like, for example, when others are enjoying themselves without you – find something else to do which is interesting and, preferably, is also energetic (such as exercising the dog, playing a game, riding your bicycle, cleaning and tidying a room or cupboard etc);
- If the loneliness seems likely to last much longer, *talk* to someone – a parent, a teacher or a relative – about how you feel. This is especially important if you feel lonely because you are being bullied;
- Try to get involved in activities which include lots of other pupils.

Remember, *you don't have to be lonely* – but it is difficult for anyone to help you unless you take the first step and tell someone how you feel. It's often a surprise when we discover just how willing people are to help us, *if they know we have a problem.*

How can we help those who are lonely?
- Be prepared to listen to them, and show understanding of how they feel;
- Help them to find other pupils with similar interests;
- Tell someone else, an adult if necessary, who may also be able to help.

It sometimes feels enjoyable to be alone. It always feels miserable to be lonely.

Things to do

1 Working in small groups, and drawing upon personal experience as far as possible, ask pupils to provide a list of situations in which pupils of their age sometimes feel lonely.

From the small group lists, collate and discuss a whole class/group list. Are some types of loneliness more common than others?

2 Pupils are asked to return to their groups and to suggest strategies whereby, in each of the situations they have listed, the lonely person might have overcome or combatted his/her loneliness.

Invite pupils to reflect privately on any occasions they have felt lonely, and to review what steps they might have taken.

3 As an individual activity, ask pupils to write an imaginary diary entry at the end of a day when they have felt particularly lonely. The entry should describe the circumstances that led to the loneliness, and should try to capture as closely as possible the feelings and thoughts experienced.

4 In an attempt to prevent burglaries, many communities have introduced a Neighbourhood Watch scheme. Ask pupils to suggest how it might be possible to introduce a Loneliness Watch scheme in school. What sort of things would be necessary to make such a scheme work?

5 *A 'loneliness' poem*:

Ask each pupil to produce a simple statement giving an example of loneliness. The statement should begin:

                Loneliness is ...

The statements should then be structured to form a class/group poem.(As a model, see Helen Wyatt's poem 'Fear', under the topic 'Fear', *Things to do*).

See also

People Need People

Alone

On a Desert Island

ALONE

Focus

To help pupils examine their ability to be self-reliant

For reflection

Imagine: It is afternoon. You are alone in the house, and will be for the next two or three hours. You have the telephone number of a neighbour whom you can call if you need to but, otherwise, you will be alone for a few hours. How do you feel?

Are you pleased to be alone so that you can do whatever you want?

Or do you hate being alone and look forward to someone returning?

Some people spend long hours alone because they really enjoy the quiet of being by themselves. Or perhaps they need to be alone because they're studying for an examination and need to concentrate hard. Others may be undertaking a strict, personal training programme in preparation for some important sporting event.

In the past, lighthouse keepers often spent weeks or months alone in the lighthouse, and religious hermits lived alone, sometimes in isolated hillside caves far from other people. Today, it is not uncommon to hear of someone who is attempting to sail around the world alone, or is rowing the Atlantic, or is walking or cycling vast distances, often to raise money for charity.

Then, of course, there are people like hostages, or prisoners, who are sometimes kept in 'solitary confinement' for long periods of time, against their wishes – locked away by themselves for days, weeks, months or even years.

But let's return to you – left alone in the house for two or three hours.

How are you going to spend the time?

Do you like silence? Can you enjoy being alone without the sound of conversation or music? Or will you need to turn on the TV or phone a friend?

Do you enjoy activities that don't necessarily involve other people – such as making things, reading, painting, playing games or using a computer, playing an instrument, solving puzzles and so on?

How will you feel if, just when you are expecting someone to return, you receive a phone call to say there has been a change of plans and you will be alone for a further hour or so?

Will you feel pleased, or will you certainly *not* look forward to even more time alone?

This, of course, is an imaginary situation. It is intended to encourage you to think about your own feelings – the sort of person you are – your strengths and weaknesses. If it were a real situation, how well do you think you would cope?

How do you think you would feel about the idea of living alone permanently?

Would there be more advantages than disadvantages, or would there be more disadvantages than advantages?

Many people *do* live alone – *not always because they have chosen to do so.*

Things to do

1 Open discussion.
   Discuss with pupils' their responses to the situation outlined.
   Would they welcome it?
   Do they enjoy times by themselves? Why?/Why not?
   How important to them is the presence of other people?
   Do they enjoy silence?
   What solitary activities or pastimes do they (not could they) engage in on a regular basis?
   How well do they think they would cope with the situation?

2 Invite pupils to devise personal timetables showing how they would be likely to use a period of three hours, as in the circumstances described.

   Working in small groups, they should then compare timetables and perhaps discuss any interesting or unusual features.

3 If pupils found themselves in the position of living alone, what personal qualities and skills do they possess that would be valuable?

   What necessary qualities and skills are they lacking, or would need to develop further?

4 With or without the assistance of pupils, compile a selection of pictures illustrating contrasting examples of the theme 'Alone'. Each picture should comprise an isolated person, but should also include sufficient background to suggest a context or location.

Working individually or in small groups, pupils should provide a brief story to explain the picture presented to them. To do this it will be necessary for them to give the character an imaginary identity – suggesting a name, age, job, family background etc. – and to describe what has led to the scene captured in the picture.

Responses to this activity become especially interesting when different interpretations of a particular picture are compared.

Pupils should also be asked to decide whether any of the characters who are alone are also lonely. (Cf. 'Loneliness')

5 Using whatever instruments are available (e.g. classroom percussion, recorders, keyboards etc.), and working either individually or in small groups of not more than three, ask pupils to create a short musical extract which captures and enhances the mood depicted in a picture (chosen by the pupil/group) from the above selection.

Points for pupils to consider include:
timbre – the selection of the appropriate type/quality of instrumental sound to match the mood;
pitch – high or low sound;
texture – how many instruments will play at any one time;
rhythm – lively and chirpy, or relaxed;
tempo – fast or slow;
dynamics – loud or soft. Will there be planned moments of silence (rests)?

It may be effective for a phrase or figure to be repeated more than once *or* the music might unfold as if illustrating a sequence of events.

As with the previous activity, responses become especially interesting when different interpretations of a particular picture are compared – and music is the most powerful medium for suggesting and changing mood.

See also
On a Desert Island

Loneliness

People Need People

A Bit of Peace

ANGER

Focus

To examine the causes and nature of anger, and to explore ways of defusing potentially volatile situations.

For reflection

Do you ever get angry?

What sorts of things make you angry? For example, do you get angry

- if someone calls you names?
- if someone threatens you, or tries to snatch something from you?
- if someone pushes in before you in the dinner queue?
- if you're trying for the umpteenth time to do something that requires a lot of patience, and you've almost succeeded when something happens and the whole thing is upset?
- when an adult treats you as if you were a baby?
- when you feel you've been treated unfairly?
- when you see someone else being treated unfairly?
- when you're in a hurry and you can't find something that's important?

Are there other things that make you angry?

What do you do when you are angry? How do you show your anger? How do you feel when you are angry? How does your body behave? Do your muscles tighten? Does your face become red? Do you suddenly feel full of energy, ready to explode?

How do you think others feel when you are angry? Does your show of anger make your relationships with others better or worse?

How do you feel when the anger has passed? Do you feel sorry? Do you feel guilty? Do you feel annoyed with yourself for getting into such a state about something that probably wasn't very important really?

Do you look back at the situation and think whether there might have been other ways of dealing with it?

This last question is an important one. Most of us, if not all, feel angry from time to time. It is natural to do so. Anger is a sign that a person feels strongly about something. But different people behave in different ways when they are angry.

Anger is a very powerful feeling. We usually can't control *when* it is going to occur – something happens which annoys us intensely and we automatically feel angry. But, even if we can't control when it is going to happen, we can, to some extent, control *how* we express our anger.

People who regularly 'lose their temper' tend to make everyone else's life miserable, and they are not well-liked nor respected. So, how can we begin to control our anger?

Perhaps the first and most practical thing we can do is to take some sort of action that will allow us to 'cool down'. 'Count to ten before you say or do anything', was the old-fashioned advice. But counting to ten is of little value unless we use that breathing space to look again at the situation and decide what is the most *appropriate* action to take – and the word 'appropriate' is important because sometimes (perhaps most times) we become angry over things which we later recognise as being trivial and of little importance. It is also helpful, if we can, to try and look at the situation from a different point of view: from the point of view held by the person or persons with whom we are angry; from the point of view of someone who is not involved, someone who is neutral, rather like a referee or an umpire.

Of course, this sort of action can only work if we are *moderately* angry. If we are *extremely* angry, we need to get away from the scene for the time being – perhaps by going to our room or somewhere where we can be alone. Alternatively we might try to distract ourselves by doing something active such as bashing a ball against a wall, or skipping. Or perhaps we might watch TV or listen to some music. It's difficult to remain angry when we get involved in something else, especially if we are gradually able to relax a little.

Whatever we do, we should try to break the succession of angry thoughts, and take time to 'cool down'. Only then will we be able think straight once more. We might even write down exactly what it is that has made us so angry, so that, later, we can think about it more carefully.

When we have cooled down we can decide whether we still feel so strongly about what happened in the first place. If we do, *now* is the time to express our feelings reasonably but clearly to the person or persons who caused us to feel angry. Generally, people respect those who express their strong feelings in a controlled way and, because of that respect, there is a far greater chance that those views will be listened to with sympathy, and it is probable that some change will come about.

Let's say again, anger is a very powerful feeling. It causes us to feel full of energy. We can either *lose* that energy by 'losing our temper', or we can *use* the energy by taking controlled action to make clear the strength of our feelings, at the right time and in an appropriate manner.

Things to do

1 Divide pupils into small groups of threes or fours. Ask the groups to suggest alternative ways of coping with each of the possible causes for anger outlined in the passage.

 Which of these are 'count ten' situations? (There are no right and wrong answers!) Are any of them likely to require more drastic action? Which is the most difficult to respond to?

 Conclude with whole class/group discussion to share and compare reponses.

2 Ask pupils to close their eyes and imagine a situation that would make them *very* angry. Ask them to try and capture exactly how they would feel and how their body would feel – how tense their muscles would be.

 Can they feel the tightness in their legs? The tension in their fingers? Their arm muscles? Their back? Their neck muscles? Their jaw? Their eyes? What would their breathing be like?

 While they are still in this state of tension, with their eyes closed, go through the same list once more, but on this occasion ask them to completely relax each muscle as it is mentioned. So they begin by relaxing the leg muscles, then the fingers, then the arms and so on.

 When they have relaxed their eyes ask them to smile gently, and then draw in and quietly release a deep breath. Now they can open their eyes.

 Tell pupils that this relaxation technique, particularly the tightening and relaxing of muscles and the deep breathing, can be adapted to soothe their feelings whenever they are anxious or tense. (See also 'Fear'.)

3 '*An angry symphony*': Using untuned and tuned percussion instruments, and working in groups of four or five, ask pupils to create a short soundscape expressing the feeling of anger. To provide the piece with shape, the opening should suggest the mood of a person feeling irritated by something or someone.

The person becomes gradually but increasingly annoyed until, eventually, the mood explodes into full blown anger, but then subsides once more as things cool down.

Points for pupils to consider include:
timbre – the selection of the appropriate type/quality of instrumental sound to illustrate the unfolding story. There will need to be contrasting types of sound;
rhythm – lively or relaxed? Spiky or smooth? Even or uneven?
pitch – high or low or both?
texture – how many instruments will play at any one time?
manner of performance – how the instruments will be played;
tempo – fast or slow or changing?
dynamics – loud or soft? Contrasts? Crescendos and diminuendos?

Although the soundscapes will be 'composed' in small groups, it will be interesting to experiment with a whole class/group performance in which individual groups enter one after another, in the manner of a round. The texture, volume, and confusion of sound and rhythm patterns will increase and recede effectively, with a little manipulation necessary in the last few bars!

If a resource stimulus is required, use a recording of the 'Storm Interlude' from the 'Four Sea Interludes' from Benjamin Britten's opera *Peter Grimes*. The music dramatically depicts the anger of a turbulent storm lashing the Suffolk coast.

Alternatively, use 'Mars' from *The Planets* by Gustav Holst. A similar insistent, pounding rhythm pattern could be incorporated in pupils' own compositions if they wished.

In either case, use only a short extract, say 2-3 minutes, and direct pupils' attention to the composer's use of the musical elements defined above i.e. timbre, texture etc.

Ask pupils to design and colour a pattern to suggest 'anger'. They should think carefully about the choice of lines and shapes (e.g. smooth and curved/angular and barbed?), and about the choice of colours. Are some colours more 'angry' than others?

See also

Fear

A Bit of Peace

FEAR

Focus

To examine some of the causes of fear, and to suggest possible paths for action.

For reflection

What frightens you? What are you afraid of?

We are all afraid of something – even though there are people who say they are afraid of nothing! Fear is nothing to be ashamed of. It is perfectly natural and sometimes protects us from possible danger. For example, a fear of drowning might discourage someone who can't swim from getting out of their depth at the seaside, or in the swimming pool. A fear of heights might discourage someone from attempting to climb a steep rock face. Can you think of examples?

Just take a few moments, and think about the thing or things you are afraid of.

Some pupils of your age say they are afraid of the dark, or of visiting the dentist, or of pain, or of being bullied, or of spiders or other insects and creepy crawlies, or of mice or rats or snakes. Some are afraid of heights, or lifts, or of swimming baths or dangerous fairground rides. Some are afraid of moving to a new school, or of being alone.

Are your fears in this list? Do you have other fears?

Of course, not all fears are equally important. For example, being afraid of snakes, or fairground rides, will not prevent anyone from living a fairly normal life. But fear of the dark, or of being alone, or of visiting a dentist, can make life very difficult.

So, what do we mean by 'fear'? *What is fear?*

To help us understand 'fear' let us ask two questions:

First, let us ask, 'Can we be afraid of something that has already happened?' The answer must be 'no'. We can't be afraid now for something that is past and over – although something that has happened in the past might make us afraid that the same thing could happen again in the future.

For example, if you had been trapped in a lift, it would not be surprising if you were not very keen to use lifts for a while. In time you would realise that lifts are, in fact, very reliable, and your experience had been a very rare and unfortunate accident. Gradually your fear of lifts would get less until it disappeared.

So, if we can't be afraid of something that has already happened, let's ask the second question, which is, 'Are we afraid of something when it is actually happening?'

Again the answer is generally 'no' – although we might be afraid of what will happen next. For example, usually the worst part of a visit to the dentist is sitting in the waiting room! And the person who says he is afraid of heights means that he is afraid of what might happen *if* he fell.

And that is the point. We are not afraid of what is happening, when it is happening. We are only afraid of what *might* happen in the future. In other words, *fear is thinking and imagining what might happen, not now but in the future.*

So what can we do about our fears?

- Some fears can be overcome by asking for the help of a sensible and reliable person – someone we trust, such as a parent or a teacher. For example, a fear of the dark, or of lifts, or of flying, can often be overcome by facing that fear with someone who has been in a similar situation many, many times before and who knows there is really nothing to be afraid of. Bit by bit a little of the other person's confidence rubs off on us and we become less and less afraid.
  Do remember, a fear of being bullied is always something to talk to a teacher or parent about.
- Sometimes we can overcome a fear by trusting what an experienced expert has to say. For example, if Sir David Attenborough brought a snake into your classroom and said, 'This snake is perfectly safe. I would like you all to stroke it,' it is likely that almost everyone would do so. Because Sir David is an expert, his word can be trusted. Similarly, if we have a fear of flying it is sometimes helpful to remind ourselves that pilots and air stewardesses fly every day as a matter of choice. It is hardly likely that they would do so if they felt their lives to be in danger.
- An effective way of easing our fear of the future, such as a visit to a dentist, is to *concentrate hard on what we are doing now*, and so *crowd out* all other thoughts, both of the future and of the past. Things seldom turn out to be as bad as we feared, and when we find

this out for ourselves we become gradually less and less afraid each time a similar experience comes along.

So, let us think about the question again. What are you afraid of? *What can you do to overcome your fear?*

Things to do

1 Working in groups of three or four, ask pupils to share, and make a list of, situations when they have been afraid. It is important that the list is based upon personal experience, and comprises various types of fear rather than quoting several illustrations based on similar situations.

   In whole class sharing, collate the information from the groups, and draw attention to the range of fears listed. Where appropriate, ask pupils to discuss ways in which particular fears might be mastered – especially if pupils are able to contribute helpful examples.

2 Either in small groups or as a whole class/group, ask pupils to discuss any differences between the fears they experience in everyday 'real' life, and those fears caused 'artificially' by, for example, horror movies.

   Do they like horror movies? Why?/Why not?

3 Ask pupils to close their eyes and imagine a situation in which they would feel very frightened. Ask them to concentrate totally on the situation and try to capture how their body would feel.

   Ask them to think about their breathing. Is the breathing irregular? Are they, for a while, holding their breath? Is the heart pounding? Is the pulse racing? Is the skin on the arms goose-pimpled? Does the scalp feel prickly? Is there a feeling of the 'hair standing on end'? Is the mouth open? Are the fingers tense? Are the finger tips placed on the lower lip?

   While they are still in this state of tension, with their eyes closed, ask the pupils to focus on their breathing, and take a long, slow, deep breath (to a count of five), breathing through the nostrils, and then exhale gently and slowly (again to a count of five). Repeat the process ten times.

   While they are continuing with an even pattern of breathing, ask pupils to be aware of any tightened muscles – such as the fingers, the neck, and the spine – and consciously relax them.

The associated symptoms – pounding heart, rapid pulse, goose pimples etc – will gradually subside.

[N.B. Breathing techniques associated with the practice of yoga use 'left nostril breathing' to 'cool' the right side of the brain where emotions such as anger, irritability, tearfulness and nervousness have their origin. To use the technique, the right nostril is closed by pressing gently on the side of the nose, and long, even breaths are inhaled and exhaled through the left nostril. The process is repeated 20 times].

4 Read to the pupils Helen Wyatt's poem 'Fear':

Fear

Fear is a lonely lane past a grave-yard.
Fear is a wood after night has fallen.
Fear is a passage in an old old house.
Fear is a terrible thing in the mind.
Fear is a slide before we are sliding.
Fear is a tree we have climbed too high.
Fear is the highest board of the swimming-pool.
Fear is a terrible thing in the mind.

Helen Wyatt

Ask each pupil to produce a simple statement giving a *personal example* of fear. As in Helen Wyatt's poem, the statement should begin:

Fear is ...

The statements should then be structured to form a class/group poem.

See also

Anger

Is There Any Body There?

SADNESS

Focus

To assist pupils' understanding of sadness – its causes and effects;

To suggest ways in which sadness can be alleviated;

To recognise the positive benefits to be derived from experiences of sadness.

For reflection

There are some things in life we would rather do without, and sadness is one of them. But, whether we like it or not, we all feel sad from time to time.

When were you last sad? What was the cause?

Often the feeling of sadness is connected with the loss of someone or something. For example:

- Have you ever felt sad about the loss of a person – perhaps caused by the death of a relative or someone you knew well? When Diana, Princess of Wales died there was a general mood of sadness throughout the country.
- Have you ever felt sad when you have seen a news item on TV reporting that someone, perhaps a child, has been killed in a road accident or fire?
- Have you felt sad at the loss of an animal?
- Have you ever felt sad because something you have said or done has caused hurt to someone?
- Have you felt sad when you have lost something that was important to you?
- Have you felt sad when you have heard adults having a row?
- Have you felt sad when you have seriously fallen out with a special friend?
- Have you ever felt sad when someone has gone away and you were unsure whether you would see them again?

What other things have made you feel sad?

When you are sad, what does it feel like? Do you ask yourself 'Why has this happened?' Do you wonder what the future will be like?

Do you feel tired and not want to do anything? Would you welcome a little sympathy and understanding from someone – a bit of affection and fuss?

Do you think about how terrible you feel?

If your answers to these last four or five questions have been mostly 'yes', then you are not unusual, and most other people would understand how you feel. We have all had similar experiences and we have had to learn how to break free from the gloomy mood of sadness.

So how can this be done?

Undoubtedly the most effective cure for sadness is *time*. When you're feeling sad it is often difficult to believe that things will ever improve, but sure enough, with the passing of hours, days, weeks and months the pain becomes less and less. Think once more about the sadness associated with the death of Diana, Princess of Wales. Although the shock and sadness caused by her death can be easily recalled, the pain and hurt experienced at the time have faded considerably.

But what can be done more immediately – at the time when the sadness is new?

The natural thing is to want to be alone, but that is not a good idea. Left alone, there is little to do except think over and over again about what has happened, and the sadness is increased rather than lessened. It helps to *talk* to someone you trust and respect – to share your feelings with them. This releases some of the pressure you feel inside – rather like gently unscrewing the cap on a bottle of Coke and letting out some of the fizz.

It is also sensible to *do* something, preferably with friends or family – something that takes your mind away from whatever is causing your sadness, and breaks the constant stream of sad thoughts.

Another remedy is to do something physical, such as playing a game or riding a bicycle – something energetic. Some use the opportunity to tackle a job that has needed doing for some time but has been put off – such as tidying a bedroom, cleaning out a pet's cage, or cleaning a bicycle, for example. Running errands for someone else helps.

As things begin to improve, two other important stages will be reached. Firstly, as you look around you will notice that their are others who are in a worse position than you, and who have greater reason for feeling sad!

Secondly, you will realise that there is a future, and you need to think what you are going to do with it.

Sadness is a 'not nice' feeling, but perhaps if we did not sometimes feel sad we would not value so greatly those occasions when we are really happy.

It's also true that our own experiences of sadness help us to understand and sympathise with others when they are going through bad times.

So perhaps sadness is something we can't really do without after all.

Things to do

1 Divide pupils into groups of three. Ask the pupils to discuss examples of sadness in their own lives saying what caused the sadness, how they reacted, how long the sadness lasted, and whether the sadness affected their lives later.

2 Following the above discussions, obtain feedback from the groups to discover the most common cause or causes of sadness across the whole class/group.

3 In whole class/group discussion, discover in greater detail how pupils feel when they are sad.

   What sorts of thoughts and ideas pass through their minds?

   Do they blame themselves?

   Who are they sad for?

   Do they sometimes feel sorry for themselves?

   Do they fear the future? Why?

   Who do they discuss their sadness with?

   Do they take steps to try and break through their sadness?

4 Using tuned and untuned percussion instruments, and working in groups of three or four, ask pupils to create a short composition expressing the feeling of sadness. To provide the piece with shape it will be helpful for pupils to choose or create a particular incident or story as a stimulus. A visual stimulus – either a still image from a newspaper, book or magazine, or a video clip without sound – often provides an effective starting point for this task.

   Points for pupils to consider include:
   tempo – fast or slow?

rhythm – smooth or uneven?
dynamics – loud or soft? Crescendos and diminuendos?
timbre – which instruments will best express the mood?
manner of performance – how will the instruments be played e.g. gently or boisterously? How many ways can they be played?
texture – how many instruments will play at any one time? Will the number vary?
pitch – if there is a melody will it move smoothly or will it leap?

If an audio stimulus is required – to create mood and atmosphere, not as a model to be copied – the 'Death of Aase' from Grieg's *Peer Gynt Suite* or Ravel's 'Pavan for a Dead Infanta' are easily accessible and suitable examples.

5 A 'sadness' poem.

Ask each pupil to produce a simple statement giving an example of sadness.

The statement should begin:

>Sadness is ...

The statements should then be structured to form a class/group poem.(As a model, see Helen Wyatt's poem 'Fear', under the topic 'Fear', *Things to do*).

See also

Fear

Anger

Happiness

HAPPINESS

Focus

To help pupils explore the causes and nature of happiness

For reflection

There is no doubt that one thing we all want is *happiness*. It doesn't matter how old or how young we are, how clever, how beautiful, how rich or how poor, we still want to be happy. In fact, we spend much of our time looking for opportunities to be happy. Happiness is a good feeling, especially when compared with those occasions when we feel sad, or bored, or annoyed with someone or something.

So what sort of things make you happy? For example:

Do you feel happy when you are with your friends – perhaps playing games or playing with toys?

Are you happy when you achieve something – perhaps when you do something well and you are praised by your teacher or parents?

Does seeing other people happy make you happy?

Does receiving presents make you happy?

Do you like giving presents? Does seeing the excited expression on the face of a person you are giving a present to make you feel happy?

Do you feel happy when you do things to help someone else and they appreciate what you've done?

Does watching comedy shows on television make you feel happy?

Are there other things that often make you feel happy?

When we are happy we feel good inside, but how else can you describe your feelings? For example:

Do you feel tired and drained, as people often do when they are sad, or do you feel lively, sparkling and bouncy?

Do you want to be alone, or do you want to be with others?

Do you feel good about other people – ready to forgive them if they've wronged you in some way?

What do you do when you are happy? How do you show your happiness?

How can you tell when other people are happy? What are the signs?

One extraordinary characteristic of happiness is that it is infectious, it is catching. It is difficult to remain miserable or sad when there is happiness around. The effect is rather like being in a totally darkened room with no window, no light, and the door shut. If someone opens the door by just two centimetres, so that a ray of light shines in, the room is no longer dark, and as our eyes become accustomed to the change, so the room seems to get lighter still.

The effect of happiness is rather like that ray of light. It brightens up the gloom.

Happiness is so important to us that people sometimes try to buy it by spending large sums of money on expensive luxury items. Unfortunately, although such things often make life more comfortable they don't necessarily make people happier – especially once the newness has worn off. Others eat and drink in search of happiness, and some turn to drugs.

But the true causes of happiness cannot be bought. Just think back to the causes discussed earlier. *The things that make us happy mostly involve sharing with other people*; they are usually quite simple, and they are always priceless – we can't go out and buy them.

We all want happiness. Fortunately, because happiness breeds more happiness, there will always be plenty to go round. Whether or not we find *happiness depends on us*, and whether *we choose* to be happy.

Things to do

1 Working in groups of three or four, ask pupils to share, and make a list of, situations that have caused happiness in their lives. It is important that the list should be based upon personal experience, and groups should try to find as many different causes for happiness as possible (i.e. they should avoid quoting several illustrations resulting from a similar cause). In whole class sharing, collate the information from the groups, and draw attention to the different types of situation leading to happiness.

2 Either in small groups or as a whole class/group, ask pupils to discuss to what extent winning the National Lottery might bring happiness, or might make happiness more difficult to achieve.

3 Ask pupils to draw a grid (or provide one for them) comprising 16 squares – 4 squares wide and 4 squares high. The overall size is immaterial.

Using only two dots for eyes and a curved line for a mouth, tell pupils to place sad faces ☹ in 15 squares, and a happy face ☺ in just one square. It doesn't matter where the happy face is placed on the grid. The purpose of the task is to graphically illustrate that the one smiling face completely transforms the overall mood (cf. the slightly opened door in the darkened room).

4 *A 'happiness' poem*: Ask each pupil to produce a simple statement giving an example of happiness, based upon personal experience. The statement should begin:

> Happiness is ...

The statements should then be structured to form a class/group poem. (As a model, see Helen Wyatt's poem 'Fear', under the topic 'Fear', *Things to do*).

5 *A 'happiness' suite*: Ask pupils to imagine they are looking down on the school playground at break time. Below, in their various friendship groups, the children are happily playing. Some are skipping, some are throwing a ball to each other, some are are playing tig/tag and are chasing around. Other groups are chattering and laughing.

Divide the pupils into small groups and ask each group to choose just one aspect, one cameo, from this panoramic picture. It doesn't matter if choices are duplicated, although it is desirable to have as wide a representation as possible.

Using tuned and/or untuned percussion instruments, each group is asked to create a short musical composition which captures the mood of the particular scene or activity they have chosen.

Points for pupils to consider include:
timbre – the selection of the appropriate type or quality of instrumental sound to match the mood. For example, which instruments might be used to capture the mood of excited chatter or laughter?
pitch – high or low sound?
rhythm – will it be even or uneven? Will it be a repeated pattern (as it might well be, for instance, for a 'skipping' composition)?
tempo – fast or slow? Or will it change?
dynamics – loud or soft? Or will there be contrasts?
texture – will all of the instruments be playing all of the time? It may be effective for a phrase or rhythm pattern to be repeated more than

once, or the music might unfold as if illustrating a sequence of events. When the small group compositions have been performed and discussed individually, it will be interesting to string them together to create a musical mosaic of the playground scene. It will also be interesting to experiment with overlapping compositions – having more than one piece playing on occasions. After all, that is life in the playground!

See also

What's in a Smile?

Radiators and Drains

Sadness

HONESTY

Focus

To discuss what we mean by 'honesty';

To identify types of dishonesty;

To consider the likely consequences of both honesty and dishonesty.

For reflection

There was once a wooden puppet who came to life as a boy, and each time he told a lie his nose became longer. You may remember – his name was Pinocchio.

How honest are you? How often would your nose grow longer? How long would it grow?

What do we mean by honesty? If a person tells lies we say he is dishonest. But is honesty just a matter of *telling* the truth – or can people *behave* in a dishonest way?

For example, is the boy or girl who cheats in a test, or on the sports field, behaving honestly or dishonestly?

Is the person who doesn't buy a television licence being honest or dishonest? (Assuming, of course, that he or she owns a television!)

Can you think of other examples of dishonest behaviour?

Is this sort of behaviour as wrong as telling lies?

A short while ago, one school carried out an experiment in which, for an hour, everyone – teachers as well as pupils – was allowed to lie or tell the truth as often as they wished. What do you think happened? What do you think was the result of the experiment?

Is it easier to trust an honest person than a dishonest one? Why?

Is it always right to tell the *whole* truth?

For example, if you have a best friend who is not particularly good looking and he or she asked 'Am I ugly?', how would you answer?

Is it sometimes kinder, and less hurtful to the other person, if we avoid giving a direct answer and find another way of answering, without telling lies? To say, 'Yes, you are ugly!' would make your friend's life miserable –

not just for the moment but, perhaps, for a long time to come. Your friend obviously has more interesting and more important qualities – otherwise he or she would not be your friend! Perhaps your friend is lively, is fun to be with, is reliable, understanding, caring, kind. These are the qualities you really like about your friend. Say so. We all like to be loved and appreciated – and it's not necessary to have film star looks to be a beautiful person.

Can you think of any other occasions when to tell the whole truth might not be helpful to another person?

How do we know whether what we are saying or doing is honest or dishonest?

We are normally guided by our *conscience* – that little voice inside us, almost like a Walkman, that tells us what is right and what is wrong. We all have a conscience – Pinocchio's conscience was Jiminy Cricket. The difficult task is learning to really *listen* to what our conscience tells us, and learning to *do* what it says. Sometimes it is easier to find excuses than to do what we should do.

We don't need a Pinocchio nose to tell us whether we are being honest with ourselves, but next time you are tempted to do or say anything which is dishonest just give your nose a little rub and check its size – you never know!

Things to do

1 Working first in small groups and then as a whole class/group, ask pupils to discuss
   - *How* are people dishonest? List the many different ways in which people lie, cheat and deceive. Think of actual examples. Remember to include small acts of dishonesty – such as conveniently forgetting to return something borrowed from a friend – as well as more dramatic crimes.
   - *Why* do people lie, cheat and deceive? List the various reasons.
   - *What* effects are acts of dishonest behaviour likely to have on
     a the person who is dishonest?
     b the people who have been deceived?

   Ask pupils, 'What do you think happened in the school where pupils were allowed to lie?'

2 The passage, *For reflection*, includes an example of a situation where to tell the whole truth might be hurtful rather than helpful.

Can pupils think of other occasions when this might be the case?

What guidelines might be used to decide whether or not to tell the whole truth?

3 Ask pupils to discuss, 'Is the information we get from newspapers, the radio and television reliable? Do advertisements always tell the truth?'

4 Encourage pupils to ask themselves
- Am I as honest as I should be?
- In what ways can I improve?

See also

Trust

Points of View

Body Language

TRUST

Focus

To raise pupils' awareness of the trust we place in others, and the trust they place in us.

For reflection

Do you ever have a secret you would love to share with someone?

Do you ever know something that you are bursting to tell someone, but it's a secret, and you don't want everyone to know?

Whom do you share your secrets with?

Of course, most secrets are about things that are not really very important. But if you had a serious problem that was worrying you, whom would you turn to?

Whose advice would you trust?

The answer is almost certainly
- Someone you like and who likes you;
- Someone who is honest and reliable;
- Someone who will willingly find time to listen, and who will want to help;
- Someone who is understanding;
- Someone who is experienced and is likely to know *how* to help.

This person is probably an adult – possibly one of your parents, or a teacher – or, at least, someone older than you.

These are typical examples of occasions when we trust other people, and we choose the people we trust because what we know about them leads us to believe they are reliable and can be trusted. They have earned our trust.

But there are many occasions every day when we trust people we don't know and have never even met. For example, when we walk along the street we *trust* that drivers of cars and lorries and buses will drive their vehicles safely along the road, and will not swerve carelessly on to the pavement. We *trust* they will obey traffic signals and pedestrian crossing signs. We *trust* that people who prepare the food we buy have taken care to see that it is free from anything that is harmful. We *trust* that when we post a letter it will arrive safely through the letter box of the person to whom it was addressed. We *trust* people to respect property that is not their own. And we could think of many more examples.

In almost everything we do, we trust other people. We have to, because the opposite of trust is distrust and suspicion – and that leads to misery and chaos. Can you imagine a school in which there were just one or two pupils who could not be trusted? Think how difficult and unpleasant life would be for everyone else.

But, of course, just as we expect to be able to trust other people they, in turn, expect to be able to trust us.

How far *can others trust you?*

- How honest are you? Do you *always* tell the truth?
- How reliable are you? If you say you will do something, do you *always* do it? If you say you will meet someone at a certain time, do you do so? Do you *always* keep your promises?
- Are you able to keep a secret? Can people tell you things and know that what they have told you will not be passed on to others?

Remember, too, that we are trusted by pets as well as by people. This short poem, about a pet cat, shows how easily that trust can be broken:

> I had a little cat called Tim Tom Tay,
> I took him to town on market day,
> I combed his whiskers, I brushed his tail,
> I wrote a label, 'Cat for Sale.
> Knows how to deal with rats and mice.
> Two pounds fifty. Bargain price.'
>
> But when the people came to buy
> I saw such a look in Tim Tom's eye
> That it was clear as clear could be
> I couldn't sell Tim for a fortune's fee.
> I was shamed and sorry, I'll tell you plain,
> And I took home Tim Tom Tay again.
>
> *Charles Causley*

Can your pet trust you? Do you find the time you should to look after your pet properly, or are there times when you just can't be bothered?

There is one final question. How far *can you trust yourself*? Can you resist temptation?

- Can you resist the temptation to tell tales about others?
- Can you be trusted to get on with your homework or instrument practice when you would rather be outside playing?
- Do you show respect for other people's property, even when there is no-one else around?

Trust is one of the most important qualities in life, especially in our dealings with other people. It is easy for us to say how we expect others to behave. The challenge is for us to be sure that we match the same high standards ourselves.

Things to do

1 Divide pupils into pairs. One pupil in each pair should put on a blindfold. It is the task of the sighted pupil to safely guide their partner around the classroom or some other 'course', avoiding all obstacles, including other pupils! The blindfolded pupil should hold his or her partner's arm near the elbow, and should walk slightly behind the guide.

   The task should be repeated with the roles reversed.

   Pupils should be encouraged to reflect on how they felt when they had to trust their partner, almost totally.

   [N.B.. This task can also be used as part of the 'Seeing' topic.]

2 Ask pupils to keep a diary for one day in which they record, briefly, situations and occasions when trust is placed in them. Remind them that trust is not just about sharing worries and secrets, but often relates to being trusted to do small things – such as getting on with homework without having to be supervised.

   Arrange a session in which pupils can compare their diary entries, and raise awareness of the range of situations when we are trusted by others.

3 Pupils should be asked to draw two diagrams. Central to each is the word 'ME', perhaps enclosed in a circle or rectangle.

   In the first diagram the pupil should encircle the word 'ME' with the names of people he or she trusts during the course of a normal day. The names should be generic rather than specific – for example, 'friends', rather than listing their names individually. Arrows should radiate out from the word 'ME' to the names in the circle.

In the second diagram the central 'ME' should be encircled by the names of those who trust the pupil. From each of the names an arrow should be targeted at the word 'ME'.

4 Working first in small groups, and later as a whole class/ group, ask pupils to discuss how they decide whether someone can be trusted. In what circumstances might they trust a person (or people) as a matter or course – without having seriously to question whether they should be trusted?

In what circumstances might they be cautious and need further proof that a person could be trusted?

5 Ask pupils to discuss, 'Are there ever any occasions when it might be right to break the trust someone has placed in you?'

See also

People Need People

Honesty

Seeing

WHAT MAKES A HERO?

Focus

To identify types of heroism;

To recognise that heroic qualities and human weaknesses sometimes exist within the same person.

For reflection

[N.B. teacher: It would be unnecessarily cumbersome to refer to he or she throughout this topic, but please make clear to pupils that hero and heroine are valued equally and, for present purposes, they can choose either.]

Do you have a hero? Most people do. In fact, some people have more than one.

Is your hero a living person, or a character from history, or in a book, film or play?

What special qualities does, or did, your hero have?

What makes someone a hero?

Does a hero have to be big and strong?

Does he have to be good looking?

Does he have to be talented and skilful?

Does he have to be brave?

Does he have to be famous?

Does he have to be rich?

Can you go to college to learn how to become a hero?

Can anyone be a hero?

Do you have to be an adult?

Does a person decide for himself that he is a hero?

Are there many reasons why different people become heroes?

If a person is once a hero for something he has done, does that mean he remains a hero for the rest of his life?

Is it possible for the same person to be both a hero and a villain (a bad guy)?

Perhaps we can begin to identify two types of hero:

The first type is the person who performs a brave act – and probably risks his own life to save others. Obvious examples are war heroes, lifeboat men, firemen and mountain rescuers. But often very ordinary people, including children, become heroes for particular acts of selfless bravery which saved the lives of others, or prevented suffering. We have all seen news items in which someone has been saved from a fire, or from drowning, by an act of heroism performed by someone else.

Perhaps you can remember actual examples?

The second type is the person with oustanding qualities or skills, who fills others with admiration, and perhaps encourages others to want to be like him.

When you have been playing, have you ever pretended to be a particular famous personality or, perhaps, a character from a film or book?

But we should be careful. Just because a person is a hero in one area of his life, it does not mean that he is to be equally admired in other aspects.

We can all think of sports personalities and pop stars who are heroes to many for their fine performances on the sports field or in the concert hall, but whose behaviour in private is often shameful and certainly not to be admired and copied!

So, let us ask again, do you have a hero? What *special qualities* does your hero have? Which of your hero's qualities would you like to possess? Does your hero have weaknesses you are grateful *not* to possess?

No doubt when he was your age, your hero sat at a table in class each day, just like you! Perhaps, some day, *you'll be someone's hero!*

Things to do

1 Construct a class/group collage comprising pictures of pupils' heroes and heroines cut from colour supplements, magazines, newspapers or any other source. The finished piece should cover as wide a range as possible and should include characters from history and/or fiction as well as living people.

2 Construct a class/group collage of news headlines related to heroic deeds collected from newspapers, magazines etc. Ask pupils to search for small acts of heroism or personal achievement/sacrifice as well as more obviously dramatic examples. Ask individual pupils to explain the story behind the headlines they have chosen and to comment on what attracted them to the story.

A supplementary task might require pupils to use headlines as a stimulus for their own creative writing or art work.

3 Ask pupils to imagine that they have been able to meet their hero or heroine in person, perhaps at a party or some similar event.

They should write a letter to a pen friend, who knows very little about the hero or heroine, describing how the meeting came about, what the person was like 'in the flesh', and what it is the pupil particularly admires about the character. If the hero or heroine also has weaknesses or faults, these should be mentioned. The pen friend should be given as true a picture as possible.

4 Ask pupils to jot down, privately, anything they have done that has given them a particular sense of achievement, success or satisfaction. It doesn't matter how large or how small the achievement was, nor does it matter whether anyone else knows about it. For example, courage in overcoming a fear is sometimes a very important achievement.

It will be helpful if pupils are willing to share some, if not all, of their responses. But be prepared to respect a pupil's right to privacy.

5 Working in small groups, ask pupils to identify as many different types and examples of heroism as possible. They should then create suitable headlines to match the examples they have chosen.

It might be appropriate to compare pupils' own headlines with those selected for Activity 2.

See also

Honesty

Trust

Radiators and Drains

Labels and Stereotypes

CARING FOR AND CARING ABOUT

Focus

To distinguish between caring *for* and caring *about*;

To plan how thoughts can be translated into actions.

For reflection

Do you have a pet – a dog, cat, horse, rabbit, hamster or goldfish maybe?

Do you sometimes help to look after a younger brother or sister?

Do you, perhaps, help an older person by running errands for them?

Do you own something that you were allowed to have on condition that you would take care of it – maybe a bicycle, or some similar item?

Can you think of anything or anyone you look after or *care for*? Is there anything or anyone you are responsible for?

What does caring for these things – what does looking after these things mean? What does it cost you?

Time? Certainly caring for a pet can take up quite a lot of time – something that is often forgotten when deciding whether to have a pet in the first place!

Effort? Yes. Cleaning a bicycle takes quite a bit of effort, and so does keeping a pet in good condition, or running errands for someone else.

Money? Maybe. It depends what it is you care for, doesn't it? Pets need food, and it's nice to buy a 'toy' from time to time with which the pet can amuse itself.

But there is another kind of caring. Let us ask a slightly different question. Is there anything in your life you *care about*? 'Caring *for*' and 'caring *about*' are quite different, aren't they? For example:

Do you care about people who are worse off, or less fortunate, than you are – maybe people who are severely disabled and have to depend on the support of those who are healthy and strong – or, perhaps, people we hear about in the news who are without food or shelter, or who have lost their homes as the result of an earthquake or war?

Do you care about the environment and the problems caused by pollution? Would you like to feel there have been real improvements in the quality of the environment by the time your children are the age you are now?

Does it upset you to see people seriously falling out, particularly friends or family? Do you care about the fighting in the world – sometimes betweeen people in the same country?

Can you do anything about these things?

On a world scale the answer is probably, no. You are not the prime minister, and you are not a world leader. But even so, your voice might be heard and might be listened to.

A few years ago, there was a small girl in Northern Ireland whose father had been killed in the violence that had been going on for many years. She learned that the President of the United States of America, the leader of the most powerful country in the world, was visiting Northern Ireland, and so she wrote to him, pleading with him to use all the power he had to bring peace to Ireland. The President was so moved by the girl's letter that, before the television cameras of the whole world, he promised to try even harder to stop the violence and to bring peace.

There is no magic wand that can be waved to solve the problems of the world – if there were, it would have been waved long ago. Instead, we have to rely on everyone, on each one of us – not just politicians and world leaders – to make sure that our tiny part of the planet is in order. We *all* have a responsibility.

So the answer to the question is 'yes' – it is possible to improve things, it is possible to bring about change, and it is possible to help others to lead happier lives.

Think for a moment. What can you do?

Perhaps you can be more aware of those who would welcome your help – the blind person wanting to cross the road; an old person struggling with shopping etc. – and feel confident enough to step forward and *do something*. Perhaps you can help the homeless and the starving by giving items you no longer need (such as toys, books, records, old clothes etc.) to a local charity shop, or by taking part in a fund-raising activity?

Help to protect the environment for the future by taking waste products such as papers, cans and bottles, to recycling collection points. And try to think of ways in which the immediate environment, at home or school or in the neighbourhood, can be made cleaner, brighter and tidier.

Perhaps you can act as peace-maker to prevent bad feeling between others from developing into name-calling or fighting.

These may seem small things and unimportant but, in fact, they can improve the lives of a great many people. *A caring act is like dropping a pebble into a pond. The ripple effect reaches far beyond where the pebble enters the water.*

What does *caring about* something cost you?

        Time? Yes.   Effort? Yes.   Money? Not necessarily.

Awareness (seeing what needs doing), *planning* how you are going to do it, getting on with doing it, and *determination* are the main requirements!

Is there anything stopping you from doing something – *today*?

Things to do

1 Provide each pupil with two sheets of paper. At the centre of each the pupil should write the word 'ME', perhaps enclosed in a circle or rectangle. One sheet will be a CARING FOR sheet, and the other a CARING ABOUT sheet.

On the CARING FOR sheet, the pupil should surround 'ME' with words or symbols which represent things, animals or people the pupil looks after, either wholly or in part. Several examples are suggested in the *For reflection* passage, but it is important for each pupil to make an individual and personal selection.

When the CARING FOR sheet has been completed, ask pupils to complete the CARING ABOUT sheet in a similar way. It is probable that some of the items will require longer descriptions or explanations than on the first sheet but, for the purposes of this diagram, ask pupils to confine themselves to symbols or brief headings as far as possible. Some of the concerns may be personal. Others will be shared by several, or maybe many, pupils.

The whole of this task should be completed in silence to encourage pupils to respond and reflect individually. There will be opportunity for discussion in the following activities.

2 Working in small groups of four to six, pupils can compare and discuss their responses recorded on the CARING FOR sheet. It is likely that there will be a sizeable core of similar entries, but any unusual or especially demanding examples might usefully be brought to the attention of the whole class.

3 The CARING ABOUT responses can be more effectively discussed in a whole class context (with the exception, of course, of any private

concerns individual pupils may have). The challenge for the teacher is to guide the discussion towards personal responsibility and what can be achieved by individual pupils, rather than focusing too much on topics that are perhaps too global and remote, and which fail to generate the motivation and energy to do something.

When the initial discussions have taken place, invite pupils to select an agreed short list of, say, three or four areas of concern they feel they would like to explore more thoroughly. Try to ensure that no more than two areas at most include fund-raising as a major activity. Others, for example, might be concerned with 'the environment' (in its many interpretations), and with serving others in various ways.

Let the class divide themselves (probably with a little guidance!) according to their particular interests and, after initial brainstorming, ask the groups to suggest a plan of action for each area. A decision should then be made concerning how many of the plans to put into action.

It is important to determine at the outset the length of time each project will be allowed to run for - including lead-in time. It is also important to plan periodic reviews to assess what progress has been made, what is working well, and what needs improving.

4 Ask every pupil to design a poster which draws attention to the topic with which he or she is concerned. The poster should:
- Attract attention;
- Make clear, through the visual images used, what is the area of concern;
- Make the person who sees the poster stop and question his or her own attitudes.

The pupil should try to use no more than three words in the poster. If it is feasible for the posters to be displayed around the school, tell the pupils before they begin that this is your intention.

5 In addition to collaborative projects, encourage pupils to make personal decisions and plans.

See also

I Wish

People Need People

Sadness

Loneliness

I WISH

Focus

To compare a 'dream' wish with an 'I want' wish;

To plan how to make a wish come true!

For reflection

If you were granted three wishes, what would they be?

Think carefully for a few moments. It is not easy to choose, and you have only three choices.

Now think more carefully about those three wishes. What have you chosen? Have you chosen wishes about you, and things for you, or do they involve others in some way?

Do your wishes want to change anything, or make things better than they are?

If your wishes came true, who do you think would benefit most?

If you could have only one wish, what would it be?

Wishes are often either *dream wishes* (which we don't really think will happen soon, if ever) or, what we might call *I wish I could have* or *I want* wishes.

In a 'dream' wish, you might wish you were a famous sportsman – say, Michael Owen, scoring goals for England. Or, you might wish you were a member of a rock band, making lots of money from records and pop videos, and being mobbed by screaming fans wherever you travelled. Or, you might wish to win the National Lottery and have lots of money to spend or give away. Or, you might wish you could cure the problem of people dying for lack of food and medicine in the poorer countries of the world. Or, you might wish that people would learn to live together peacefully, and that there would be no more killing through violence and fighting. These are 'dream' wishes.

'I want' wishes, are usually about things we want to own: 'I want more pocket money; another football strip; more clothes; a dog; a better bicycle – and why can't we live in a bigger house, like Lucy's parents?'

'I want' wishes never seem to end. When we get what we want, we are satisfied for only a short while, and then we want again – something bigger, something better and, usually, something more expensive. Eventually we find that we have many toys, books, clothes, video games and so on, that are very rarely used, and that spend most of the time in cupboards and drawers. We only *think* we know what we want.

There is a fairytale told about an old lady who lived in a vinegar bottle. She was a miserable old lady who seldom smiled, and who was forever complaining that her neighbours had nicer homes, nicer clothes and ate nicer food than she could afford.

One day, when the old lady was muttering to herself and complaining about everyone and everything, a good fairy tapped on the vinegar bottle. 'What is the matter?' the fairy asked.

The old lady began to describe all the things that were making her miserable – she didn't have many friends, her home wasn't as nice as other people's and … But the good fairy interrupted her.

'Look,' said the fairy, 'I can give you three wishes, but only three'.

So the old lady wished that she lived in a beautiful cottage with a thatched roof, roses growing round the door, and a garden full of beautiful flowers. Immediately, her wish was granted and she found herself outside a beautiful country cottage. It had a thatched roof. It had roses round the door and a garden full of foxgloves and poppies and hollyhocks and lavender and rosemary and birds singing excitedly to each other in the trees, and every day the sun shone.

But very soon the old lady tired of the cottage and she complained to the fairy that everyone lived too far away, it was too quiet and she had to do everything for herself.

'Very well,' said the fairy, 'you have two other wishes. What would you like to wish?'

'I wish I lived in a palace,' said the old lady.

And no sooner had she made the wish than she found herself in a magnificent palace, complete with lots and lots of servants, all in uniform, just waiting to do whatever the old lady wished them to do.

But very soon the old lady became bored with the palace, because there was nothing for her to do – and she couldn't stand so many people fussing around her the whole time.

'Very well,' said the fairy, 'you still have one wish left. What would you like to wish?'

'I wish I could go back to my vinegar bottle,' said the old lady. And immediately her wish was granted.

Sometimes, like the old lady, we only *think* we know what we want.

A big difference between 'dream' wishes and 'I want' wishes is that 'dream' wishes at first seem to be impossible, but with 'I want' wishes we often work out ways of getting what we want – perhaps by dropping hints to parents about what we would like as a birthday present, or perhaps by doing jobs that earn extra pocket money, or by selling unwanted toys in a car boot sale, and so on. The point is *we do something about it* because *we want* something.

Sometimes, when we can change 'I wish I could' into 'I want to', even 'dream' wishes can come true.

A few years ago, at the end of a long flight to Bangladesh, a British Airways air stewardess visited a small village near Dhaka, the capital of Bangladesh. Conditions in the village were dreadful. There was little food, children were dying from hunger and disease and, of course, there was little opportunity for children to learn. The stewardess, Patricia Kerr, thought a great deal about what she had seen. Her feeling of '*I wish* I could help' became '*I want* to help', and then came the important question, '*How* am I going to help?' She told her story to other air crew staff and then to British Airways officials. With their approval, she was able to make collections among passengers on flights, and in a short while, enough money was raised to provide food, a school and medical support, sufficient to vastly improve the lives of the villagers and to bring smiles back to the children's faces.

Patricia Kerr might not have solved the world's problems for the poor and dying, but in one small village she had made a very, very important difference not just through wishing, but *through doing*.

Often when we make a wish we don't expect it to come true, and so we don't try hard enough for long enough to make it happen. Becoming very good at anything, or succeeding in something that is really worthwhile, requires perseverance – 'stickability', as it is sometimes called – and self-discipline.

Think again about your three wishes. Is there anything you *wish* to achieve? Is there anything you *want* to change? Is there anything you care about so much that you are going to try and *make it happen*? *How* are you going to do it?

Many things are possible when we are determined to succeed.

Things to do

1 Ask pupils – using pencil and paper, and working individually – to follow through the sequence of activities outlined at the beginning of the *For reflection* passage.

That is:
- Make a choice of three wishes;
- Reflect on the nature of those wishes, noting in particular:
  – whether they are 'I want' wishes or 'dream' wishes;
  – whether they involve other people;
  – whether they are wishes for change and improvement;
  – if the wishes were granted, who would benefit?

If the pupil could have only one wish, what would it be?

2 Ask each pupil to write their 'special' wish on a slip of paper, without adding his or her name, and then drop the paper into some form of receptacle provided by you – your 'wishing well'.

How you use this information will depend upon the nature of the responses. If, under the promise of anonymity, some pupils have submitted 'private' wishes, it is important that their privacy should be respected and guarded. However, it is likely that there will be similar wishes from several pupils and useful observations and teaching points can be made.

3 When the first activity has been completed, pupils should discuss their choices with a partner and, with the partner's help, should begin to develop an 'action plan' that might help a chosen wish come true. In some cases it might prove helpful, after a short while, to combine two pairs to form a foursome and perhaps stimulate further ideas.

When making an action plan pupils might find the following guidelines helpful:

(i) Set a period of time, by the end of which it is hoped or expected that the target will have been reached. The length of that period will vary according to what the pupil is trying to achieve. For example, if the wish is to master a particular skill, the period could require weeks, months, or even years. If, on the other hand, the wish is to mend a misunderstanding with a friend, the period might be much shorter.

Whatever the period is it should be divided into three – short term, medium term, and long term – with 'milestones' at the end of each, marking what can reasonably be expected to have been achieved at that point.

The first steps are vitally important and should be taken without delay. The first 'milestone' should be fairly easy to reach. This provides an early sense of achievement and provides the motivation for the next stage.

(For target-setting, see also 'Life is Not a Video Recorder,' *Things to do*.)

(ii) Most challenges are more easily managed with the support of another person or persons – someone to give encouragement when spirits are low and nothing seems to be happening.

(iii) The wish should be written down and placed in a position where the pupil's attention will be regularly drawn to it (beside a bedroom mirror is often a good place).

4 *'Who can I write to?'* Ask pupils to decide who they think is the *key person*, or the most influential person, who can make their wish come true. The pupil should then draft a letter to that person, saying
- what the wish is;
- why it is important;
- how the pupil would like the person to help;
- what the pupil him or herself is doing about it.

Of course, the key person may well be the pupil or, even, God. That's fine! The letter should still be written. Indeed, such letters often provide ideal opportunities for focused reflection and meditation.

See also

Caring For and Caring About

Freedom

Life is Not a Video Recorder

The Amazing World of Mankind

Thinking

FREEDOM

Focus

To identify constraints on personal freedom;

To consider the difference between *freedom from* and *freedom to*.

For reflection

'I want to be free!'

We all feel that way from time to time, don't we – especially when we're having to do something we don't enjoy doing and it's a beautiful day outside! But what do we mean by being 'free'? What do we mean when we speak of 'freedom'?

Some would describe freedom as 'being able to do what you want'.

Are you able to do what you want when you want? What prevents you? For example, are you restricted by people – if so, who are these people? Are they adults who have a responsibility for you and for your safety – people such as parents or teachers?

Are they younger brothers or sisters you are sometimes asked to look after? Are they, perhaps, elderly relatives who have errands to be run or odd jobs to be done?

Do you sometimes feel you have too many bosses?

Listen to John Cunliffe's poem, called 'Orders of the Day'. Does any of this sound familiar to you?

Orders of the Day

> Get up!
> Get washed!
> Eat your breakfast!
> That's my mum,
> Going on and on and on and on and on …

Sit down!
Shut up!
Get on with your work!
That's my teacher,
Going on and on and on and on and on ...

Come here!
Give me that!
Go away!
That's my big sister,
Going on and on and on and on and on ...

Get off!
Stop it!
Carry me!
That's my little sister,
Going on and on and on and on and on ...

Boss
Boss
Boss
They do it all day.
Sometimes I think I'll run away,
But I don't know where to go.

The only one who doesn't do it,
Is my old gran.
She says,
'Would you like to get washed?'
Or
'Would you like to sit on this chair?'
And she listens to what I say.

People say she spoils me,
And that she's old-fashioned.
I think it's the others that spoil;
Spoil every day.
And I wish more people were old-fashioned,
... like my gran.

Maybe you feel restricted by rules – if so, what rules? By rules at school? By rules at home?

Are you restricted by laws – if so, what laws? Is there anything you might want to do, but which the law says is wrong?

Can you think of anything else that prevents you from doing what you want?

But before you begin to feel too sorry for yourself, ask the question, 'Are there people who have less freedom than me?'

Who are they? In what ways are they restricted?

For example, can you think of people whose freedom is restricted by their health, or by some form of disability?

Or people whose freedom is restricted by their age? Or by their lack of money? Or by the colour of their skin?

Then, too, there are

- hostages, captured by terrorists and threatened with death if the terrorists' demands are not met;
- prisoners, who have had their freedom taken away as a punishment for their crime;
- refugees made homeless by war – and we have seen many pictures of frail and frightened people, struggling along mountain tracks, carrying on their backs everything they possess.

If you had total freedom, how would you use it? What would you do? Can you be sure that what you might choose to do wouldn't interfere with the freedom of others?

How might you use your freedom to help others?

Who would you want to help? In what ways?

Is there really anything preventing you from helping them now?

Sometimes, when we don't get on with something, the real reason is to be found in *the excuses we make to ourselves*. It has nothing to do with lack of freedom.

We are fortunate. We have more *freedom* than most people in the world. We need to use it sensibly and responsibly – to *help* others, to *care* for the world we live in, and to *make ourselves better people*.

Things to do

1 The first half of the *For reflection* passage directs pupils' thoughts towards restrictions on freedom:
   a people, circumstances or rules/laws that in some way constrain the pupil's own freedom;
   b other people's lack of freedom, especially when the cause is totally beyond their control.

   Divide pupils into small groups and, using the questions in the passage as a guide, ask them to discuss each of these aspects, giving specific examples where possible.

   [A supplementary homework task might require pupils, during the course of the next week, to note (and possibly collect appropriate cuttings) examples in the news, especially in relation to (*b*)].

   Examples discussed by small groups should be shared with the whole class and, if possible, should be summarised in separate visual displays.

2 In whole class discussion, where appropriate relate the theme of 'freedom' to work pupils are doing in other subject areas – for example, attitudes to freedom in the Victorian age.

3 Ask pupils to keep a detailed personal diary covering a complete weekend that is, a period of maximum personal freedom.

   The information collected can be used by the pupil for a variety of purposes but, in particular, they should be asked to consider why they chose to do certain things in preference to others. Perhaps they have more freedom than they realise!

4 Possibly working in small groups, ask pupils to research the lives and work of important historical figures such as Gandhi, Martin Luther King, Nelson Mandela, William Wilberforce etc.

   Pupils should then make a presentation to the rest of the class.

5 *a* The question 'If you had total freedom, how would you use it?' clearly requires an individual response, but it is important for pupils to consider how far the exercising of their freedom might interfere with the freedom of others (for example, noise!).
   b Pupils should also examine whether they already have the freedom to do these things, but delay by making excuses to themselves. A reference back to Activity 3 might be useful.

   c In relation to the final section of the passage, encourage pupils to make a personal commitment to undertake, during the week ahead, at least one task relating to each of the identified areas i.e., 'to help others, to care for the world we live in, and to make ourselves better people'.

6 Ask each pupil to produce a simple statement giving a *personal example* of freedom. The question for each pupil to answer is 'What is my idea of freedom?' The statement should begin:

Freedom is …

The statements should then be structured to form a class/group poem.

(As a model, see Helen Wyatt's poem 'Fear', under the topic 'Fear': *Things to do*).

See also

Rules and Commandments

Caring For and Caring About

I Wish

A Bit of Peace.

A BIT OF PEACE

Focus

To raise pupils' awareness of the importance of creating opportunities for quiet and for reflection in the pattern of everyday life.

For reflection

'Will you please let me have a bit of peace!'

No doubt you have had those words said to you at some time! But what do they mean?

How would you describe what is meant by the word 'peace'?

Peace is one of those strange words we all think we know the meaning of but, when we are asked for an example, we might each suggest something very different.

For a mum and dad, peace might be that precious time in the evening when all of the jobs for the day have been completed, and the children are all tucked up soundly in bed.

Dad's idea of peace might be sitting on the bank of a river or stream, fishing. Or he might enjoy tinkering, uninterrupted, under the bonnet of the car, or pottering around, tidying the garden.

If you asked your grandparents for their understanding of 'peace', it is likely they might say, 'Peace means not being at war, not fighting.' During their lifetime there have been several wars around the world in which many, many thousands of people have lost their lives, and millions have lost their homes and all they possessed. And so, for your grandparents, 'peace', meaning 'not being at war', is something very special.

But how about you – what is your idea of peace?

Is it, perhaps, taking the dog for a walk?

Is it being alone in your room, listening to your favourite music, or reading a favourite book?

Is it not being pestered by a brother or sister?

Is it being by yourself, kicking a ball against a wall?

Is it going for a ride on your bicycle or, maybe, on a pony?

Do you have a favourite place where you can get 'a bit of peace'?

If we stop to think about all these various examples of peace we notice that, although they are different from each other, there are certain things they have in common:

Firstly, peace means *change*, in the sense of breaking away from all the activity that has been going on – a bit like free-wheeling downhill on a bicycle after the struggle of climbing to the top.

Secondly, peace means that for a while the pressure is off. In the case of war, it means that the fighting has stopped. For you and me, peace is a time when
- no-one is bossing us about – telling us what to do;
- no-one is nagging us to 'get on with it', now!
- no-one is interfering in what we're doing;
- no-one is disturbing us.

And, thirdly, 'a bit of peace' provides a 'breathing space' during which we can sort ourselves out, and think back over things we have said or done and consider whether they were the right things to say and do. We can smile to ourselves about moments we have enjoyed, and we can plan how we might deal with things we need to do in the near future.

It's rather like going on a long walk and, after a few miles, stopping to take a rest while we look at the map to see the route we have come along so far, and the route we need to take now. Sometimes, of course, we don't need to look at the map. We feel fairly confident about the route we're taking, and we're content just to take a break and enjoy the scenery.

For each of these three reasons, we all need 'a bit of peace' every day of our lives. Mum needs a break from the endless stream of responsibilities that are part of family life, not to mention the questions, 'Mum, where's this?' 'Mum, where's that?' 'Can I this?' 'Can I that?' Dad needs the opportunity to relax peacefully away from the pressures of his life too. And so do you. You need to find a few moments each day that are yours, a few moments when you press the pause button on the busy part of your life.

Often, when we've enjoyed 'a bit of peace' we seem to feel better in ourselves and about ourselves – almost as if we've taken on a fresh supply of energy. We also tend to feel more relaxed and more friendly towards other people.

If everyone would take a daily dose of 'a bit of peace', think how much happier the world might be!

Things to do

1 This activity takes pupils on a journey, in their imagination, to a place that is quiet, peaceful and safe. Once they have experienced the journey it will be possible for pupils to return to the same spot if, and whenever, they wish. It is important to stress that this is *not* a *real* journey, but takes place *only in the imagination*, just as events that occur in a story are not real but are captured in the imagination. The second point to stress is that both the journey and the place reached are *safe*.

The description of the journey, given below, requires pupils to make their own choices (to accommodate different personal experiences and preferences), and pauses are indicated (i.e. ...) after each suggestion to allow pupils to experience different situations.

Ask pupils to close their eyes and sit comfortably, with feet planted firmly on the floor and hands held loosely in the lap. Remind pupils that, except for your voice, there must be silence. When pupils are sitting comfortably, establish a relaxed state with a few controlled deep breaths. (For more detail of relaxation techniques see 'Is There Any Body There?' *Things to do*.)

THE JOURNEY:

'Keeping your eyes gently closed, listen to the words as we go on a short journey to a peaceful place, where you can rest for a few moments and be quiet and thoughtful.

See yourself now, in your mind's eye, getting up from your seat and walking out of the room ...

You are going out of the school now ...

Follow the road or path in whichever direction you choose ...

Imagine now that the road is becoming smaller and less wide ... and you are going further and further down a path or road that is leading to a place where you know you can be quiet, safe and alone for a few minutes.

Maybe your path is taking you in your imagination to your own secret place, or to a park, or through a wood, or to a green meadow ...

Be aware of how the sounds of traffic and other noises are getting fainter and fainter as you walk further along your path ...

How are you entering your place, is there a gate? ...

It is very safe and secret here. What is the place like? ...
What sort of things do you have in your safe place? ...
Take a look around. What can you see and hear? ...
Can you hear birds singing? ... Can you hear a stream? ...
Can you find a spot to sit quietly? ...
How do you feel about this place? ...
You can stay here as long as you want. Only you have the right to visit here ... Others can only come with your permission ...
Have the feeling that you can come back whenever you want ...

Now try to hold on to these feelings as you return back slowly along the path that brought you here ...
Return through the point where you entered ...
As you walk along the path be aware of the sound of the traffic and other noises becoming very gradually louder ...
Your path is becoming wider .... and you enter the road that leads to the school ... You enter the school ... and walk to your classroom ...
You go back to your seat ... and, very gently, you open your eyes.
Your journey is over.'

Allow time for *pupils to talk about where they went* and what they experienced. This is very important. It allows the experiences to evaporate and eases pupils back into the everyday world. *It should not be rushed or glossed over*. Everyone will have had a different experience and will enjoy talking about it.

2 Using small group or whole class discussions, ask pupils to share examples of peaceful moments they have particularly enjoyed, and/or methods they have used for creating 'a bit of peace' in their lives.

3 Ask each pupil to produce a simple statement giving a personal example of peace. The question for each pupil to answer is, 'What is my idea of peace?' The statement should begin:

                Peace is ...

The statements should then be structured to form a class/group poem.(As a model, see Helen Wyatt's poem 'Fear', under the topic 'Fear', *Things to do*.)

4 Ask pupils to create a pattern or abstract design that suggests an atmosphere of peace. They should think carefully about the shapes and lines they will use – for example, will the shapes be smooth or angular, will the lines be curved or jagged – and they should consider which colours might create the right atmosphere.

5 Working in groups of four or five, and using whatever instruments and sound sources are available, ask pupils to create a musical composition or soundscape as incidental music to the journey described in Activity 1, or a piece based on some similar stimulus.

Points for pupils to consider include:
timbre – the selection of the appropriate type or quality of instrumental sound to match the atmosphere;
pitch – high or low sound;
melody – if there is melodic shape, will it be smooth or will it leap around?
rhythm – will it be even or uneven? Will there be a repeated pattern such as an ostinato?
tempo – fast or slow?
dynamics – loud or soft?
texture – how many instruments will be used? Will all of the instruments be playing all of the time, or might solo instruments and pairs of instruments be used effectively?

Will some form of scoring be used (e.g. notation, graphic score etc.) to allow the piece to be performed on more than one occasion?

See also

Silence and Sound

Honesty

Freedom

I Wish

CURIOSITY

Focus

To encourage pupils to be aware of, and curious about, the world around them;

To provide practice in increasing understanding and knowledge through asking how? and why? questions.

For reflection

I wonder why the sky is blue on a hot summer's day? Why isn't it yellow, or pink or green?

If the earth is round, why don't the people in Australia fall off?

Why do cows eat green grass yet produce white milk?

How does a television picture travel through the air, through an aerial and along a cable to appear on my television screen?

How are some birds able to fly thousands of miles south to warmer countries during our winter, and then return in the summer – often to the same lake, woodland, or even to the exact building they left a few months earlier?

When we ask ourselves – or when we ask someone else - questions of this kind, we say we are '*curious*'.

Curiosity is wanting to know something, or wanting to find out. And when we want to find out we often use one of two words - they are 'How?' and 'Why?'

Perhaps you remember questions you asked when you were younger. The questions small children ask are sometimes not easy for parents to answer:

'Mummy, how do ladybirds get their spots?'

'Daddy, why is it called a ladybird? It's not a bird, and they can't all be ladies'.

Even when we are very young we understand that asking questions will help us to find out – will help us to learn. We are curious – we want to know.

We often use 'how' questions to find out how something works, how it is made, or when we want to know how to do something:
- How did the magician make the lady disappear and then come back again?
- How are electric light bulbs made?
- How can I draw a horse?

We mostly ask 'why' questions when we want someone to explain why people or things behave the way they do:
- Why does my dog, Shep, always snarl when the postman calls, but wag his tail when he sees the milkman?
- Why do babies sleep all the time?

'*How* did he do that?' and '*Why* did he do that?' are quite different questions, aren't they? So too are questions like '*How* did you get here?' and '*Why* did you come?'

We can ask 'how' or 'why' questions about almost anything. Let's try. For example:

Imagine that you have in front of you a newspaper – it doesn't have to be a particular newspaper, any newspaper will do. Try to think of at least ten 'how' questions that would help you find out more about the newspaper. (How is the news collected? How is the newspaper printed? How does it reach the homes of the readers? etc.) Try to ask interesting and searching questions that require more than just one word answers.

Now try to do the same thing asking 'why' questions.

(Why do people buy newspapers? Why are there so many different newspapers? etc.)

It is likely that you have already started to learn something about the newspaper, because to help you decide what questions to ask, you have had to think about the newspaper more carefully than you might otherwise have done.

How? and Why? have three helpful cousins called Where? When? and Who?

Being curious and asking questions – such as how? why? where? when? and who? – is an important first step when we want to know something, when we want to find out. Then, of course, we have to follow the question by doing whatever is necessary to discover the answer.

So, if the earth is round, why don't the people in Australia fall off? Can you find out?

Things to do

1 *The 'newspaper' activity:* The purpose of this activity is to demonstrate that what we find out depends upon the questions we ask. By using only how? and why? type questions pupils will become familiar with the nature of the responses these questions evoke.

Not only are some questions more interesting than others, they also lead to a more productive seam of understanding and knowledge. It is suggested that the activity is undertaken in small groups, but that the questions devised by the groups are discussed by the whole class to determine which are likely to elicit the most useful and interesting information.

Whether or not questions are pursued to the answer stage is for you to decide, but attention should be focused primarily on *seeking out searching questions* – especially those that require more than a one word answer! Where appropriate, encourage the use of related supplementary questions to explore the topice of interest in greater depth. A 'newspaper' has been chosen as an item familiar to everyone. With encouragement, pupils should be able to generate dozens of questions. But, for the purposes of this activity, any suitable object can be substituted, e.g. a tin of sardines, a supermarket trolley, a tube of toothpaste, a CD player.

Alternatively, or in addition, ask pupils to prepare how? and why? questions they would like to ask a famous person, such as the prime minister – or someone of their own choosing.

2 The 'newspaper' activity can be taken further by choosing one article or one picture from an actual newspaper, and inviting pupils to frame how? and why? questions.

There will be numerous opportunities for applying the process in various learning contexts.

3 *A 'how?' or 'why?' diary:* Within a given period of time, say 24 hours, pupils should list situations that have prompted them to ask how? or why?

It is also helpful to discuss 'missed opportunities' – occasions when questions might have been asked but weren't.

4 A 'how?' or 'why?' poem: Here is a poem by Eric Finney called, appropriately, 'Questions':

Questions

How far are the stars?
How deep are the caves?
Are there men on Mars?
What makes waves?
Why is sky blue?
Where does it end?
What makes a rainbow?
Why does it bend?
Are there really ghosts?
Why does it snow?
So many questions,
So much to know.

Perhaps using the poem as a stimulus, pupils should be invited to contribute their own 'big' how? or why? questions – things that puzzle them. Suggestions should be shared and discussed with the whole class, and perhaps structured to create a 'Questions' class poem for wall display – presenting the classroom as a cavern of curiosity, a learning zone where children are curious, where questions are asked and ideas are shared. When appropriate, the poem can be added to from time to time.

See also

The Amazing World of Mankind

The Wonderful World of Nature

Other Worlds

THE AMAZING WORLD OF MANKIND

Focus
To reflect on the amazing capabilities of man's imagination – relating to the past and the future.

For reflection
It's almost unbelievable, isn't it, that a huge aeroplane with 360 passengers (and their luggage) on board, can fly to the south of Spain in less than 3 hours. How does such a monstrously heavy load take off and become airborne? How does it fly at a speed of almost 600 miles per hour – that is, ten miles in one minute? And how, at the end of its journey, does it manage to descend gradually from a height of 37000 feet (7 miles), to land gently on a tarmac runway? It's amazing!

To design, build and fly such an aircraft is a truly incredible achievement, and yet such journeys occur so frequently every day that we take them for granted. To many people even Concorde, which can travel at twice the speed of sound, is just another fast aeroplane! Can you imagine that – 1350 miles per hour? That's amazing!

All corners of our lives are being constantly affected by new inventions, by new developments in technology, and by the latest discoveries in science. But sometimes ideas that are very helpful are also very simple – so simple, in fact, that we wonder why they have not been thought of before! The use of 'cats' eyes' to mark the middle of the road for night drivers is a good example. So was the introduction of bread that was already sliced. But however simple or clever an invention seems to be, it almost always starts with the question 'What if?'

Those great aeroplanes of today have developed from a question asked hundreds of years ago: 'What if a man could fly like a bird?' More than 500 years ago, the great painter Leonardo da Vinci (who was also an architect, an engineer, and a scientist) designed a flying machine. And we have all seen films of men, four centuries later, with large wings fastened to their arms, jumping from cliff tops and seaside piers. They look rather comical to us now, but they show man's determination to fly like a bird and, of course, through perseverance, he has succeeded.

Similarly, the question 'What if man could fly to the moon?' became a possibility and, in 1969, Neil Armstrong became the first person to set foot on the moon.

The question 'What if it were possible to give a person a new heart?' was answered in 1967 when the South African surgeon, Christiaan Barnard, performed the first heart transplant operation.

In New York, towards the end of the nineteenth century, land became so scarce and so expensive that architects asked themselves 'What if we make our buildings stretch upwards instead of sideways?' And so they began to design buildings so tall they seemed to scrape the sky, and they became known as 'skyscrapers'. For many years, the tallest skyscraper was the Empire State Building, built in 1931. It has 102 storeys and is 381 metres (1250 feet) high. That is more than 40 times the height of an average house! Then, in 1973, the Sears Tower was built in Chicago to an amazing height of 443 metres (1454 feet).

These are just a few ways in which the 'What if?' question has led to remarkable achievements. And, of course, we are surrounded by millions of other examples, most of which we use without stopping for a second to appreciate how truly amazing they are.

Just pause for a moment now and ask yourself, of all the inventions and discoveries made during the last fifty years, which have made the greatest difference to the way people live. Think, for example, of types of transport and travel, types of communication (some using satellites in space), the inroduction and use of computers including personal PCs, and so on.

Which inventions or discoveries have made the greatest difference to the way people live?

Is there anything that makes you feel 'I would love to have invented that' or 'I would love to have discovered that'?

Now think ahead 50 years. How different do you imagine the world will be then?

Will your grandchildren go to school each day in the way you do?

Will people still drive around in cars?

Will people go shopping at weekends?

What sort of things would you like to see happen? Can you think of a few 'What if?' questions you would like to present as a challenge to scientists, inventors, doctors and designers? Remember that 'What if?' questions always take a big step beyond what is possible at the present time.

Of course, an idea, however exciting it may be, is of little value unless someone believes that it *can* be done, it can be achieved, and is determined to persevere to *make it happen*. There are always doubters – those who say 'It won't happen. It can't be done'. But the names of the doubters are soon forgotten. These people are not the ones who improve the lives of others.

There is a poem called 'It can't be done' which says:

> The man who misses all the fun
> Is he who says, 'It can't be done'.
> In solemn pride he stands aloof
> And greets each venture with reproof.
> Had he the power he'd efface
> The history of the human race;
> We'd have no radio or motor cars,
> No streets lit by electric stars;
> No telegraph nor telephone,
> We'd linger in the age of stone.
> The world would sleep if things were run
> By men who say, 'It can't be done'.
>
> *William J Bennett*

As long as men and women, and boys and girls, continue to ask 'What if?' and use imagination and perseverance to answer their questions, remarkable inventions and discoveries will be the result; exciting stories, poems, paintings and musical compositions will continue to be created, and the world will remain a fascinating and amazing place.

Things to do

1 Working in small groups, ask pupils to discuss inventions that have taken place and discoveries that have been made during the last 50 years or so. Using the criterion, 'Which have made the greatest difference to the way people live?' ask each group to produce a short list of *five* choices. In whole class/group sharing, the lists of the various groups can be compared and discussed.

Encourage pupils to consider the 'before and after' situations associated with the choices they make.

2 To raise pupils' awareness and appreciation of developments in their immediate environment, the previous task can be repeated using a specific focus, such as
>   the home environment
> *or* the school environment
> *or* the town or village in which the school is situated.

3 Working in small groups, ask pupils to discuss inventions and discoveries they would like to see happen in the future. What changes would they like to see? Can they devise 'What if?' questions that might help to bring about such changes?

The contributions of the small groups can be compared and discussed in a whole class/group session.

4 *Theme park: 'The shape of things to come'.* The task is to construct a whole class/group collage illustrating and describing life in the year 2050. Using the 'theme park' principle, it will be helpful to first decide on a list of areas of life to be covered, such as:
Home; School; Work; Entertainment; Holidays; Shopping; Health/Medicine; Transport; Communications; Childhood; Old age, and so on.

Because of the futuristic nature of the task, the range of available 'ready-made' images may be limited – encouraging pupils to rely on their own designs and imagination.

In addition to illustrations, the collage might include diary extracts written in the year 2050 by a range of people (including the pupil at the age of 60-ish), journalists' reports on imaginary incidents and happenings, descriptions of television programmes or news bulletins etc.

See also

What If?

Curiosity

The Wonderful World of Nature

Other Worlds

THE WONDERFUL WORLD OF NATURE

Focus

To encourage pupils to reflect on the wonderful, the amazing, the beautiful and the mysterious, in the world of nature.

For reflection

'I wonder what he's up to?'

There is something about the word *wonder* that somehow suggests mysterious or secretive goings-on!

When we say, 'I wonder how?' or 'I wonder why?' it is almost as if we're trying to uncover some deeply guarded secret, or solve a mysterious puzzle. 'I wonder?' means I'm asking myself the question. I want to find an answer that satisfies me.

But sometimes, in the world of nature, we are excited by something unexpected, or strange, or unusual and we just want to enjoy the magic of what is happening. For the time being, we don't really want an explanation of 'how' or 'why' – that might spoil the *wonderful* moment. Later, maybe, but not at that moment.

For example, imagine a particularly beautiful sunset, or a rainbow. An explanation at that time of how the effect is created in the atmosphere, however interesting it may be, is unlikely to increase the actual enjoyment of the experience.

On other occasions we might see something amazing that immediately causes us to ask questions. For example, if we see a procession of ants crossing our path we are curious to find out where they have come from, where they are going to, and what they are carrying.

Or if we see a bird's nest in a tree, we might wonder how the bird began to build the nest. How did it know where to place the first twig or first piece of straw so that it would not fall? How did it secure those first pieces of building material to make them safe against the wind and the movement of the tree?

How does the spider begin to build its beautifully patterned web? How does it draw its first threads across the huge space between the two posts, or whatever the spider has chosen to support the web?

Can you think of any occasions when something in nature has caused you to say to yourself, 'That's *wonderful*!' Or, 'That's *amazing*!'?

Nature is very beautiful in countless, contrasting ways – from breathtakingly impressive mountain scenery, to the spotted wings of the ladybird; from the cuddly playfulness of young animals to the savage pounding of a rough sea against a rocky shore; from the perfect form of the tiniest flower to the vast empty spaces of the desert.

Sometimes, faced with an endless stretch of sea, or standing by a prehistoric rock, or listening to the continuous roar of a gigantic waterfall, we can feel very small, very helpless and very unimportant. These things were here long before we arrived on earth and, no doubt, will be here long after we have gone.

The world of nature is always fascinating. Sometimes we want to ask 'I wonder how?' or 'I wonder why?'

But there are other times
- when it is more satisfying just to really enjoy the *amazing*, the *wonderful*, the *beautiful* and, perhaps the *mysterious* things around us;
- when there are no words that can truly describe *what we feel inside*;
- when we should be grateful that we have the opportunity to enjoy such *magic moments*.

Then, deep within ourselves, we might wonder, '*How did it come to be like this?*'

Things to do

1 Provide a suitable display area in the classroom where pupils can exhibit their found natural objects e.g. pebbles, shells, interesting leaves, feathers, nuts, driftwood sculptures.

   Encourage interest in the collection and, where suitable, use the objects for observational drawing – thereby requiring pupils to become more aware of the features, characteristics and qualities of the items.

2 Ask pupils to describe, either orally, in writing, or through pictorial composition, a favourite area of natural beauty – or the type of natural environment they most enjoy.

3 To increase awareness of insects and creatures they are likely to meet fairly frequently, ask pupils to find out all they can about the following, and produce fact sheets to help those who are less knowledgeable:

        ant   bee   wasp   housefly   spider   snail

4 Similarly, to encourage visual awareness, ask pupils to find out more about regular visitors to the garden:
a birds: blue tit/great tit   chaffinch   robin
Provide outline drawings of the birds and ask pupils to colour them appropriately.
b butterflies: small tortoiseshell   peacock   red admiral
Again, provide outline drawings and ask pupils to colour in the distinctive markings.

5 Ask pupils to answer the following questions, basing their responses on *personal experiences only*:

'The things I think are beautiful are ...'
(Remember to include things that are beautiful to touch, to listen to, or to taste, in addition to those that are beautiful to look at, watch, or see)

'The things I think are amazing/wonderful are ...'
(Remember to include anything relating to animal behaviour, things seen through a microspope or telescope etc.)

'Things I find mysterious are ...'
(These might include places or, for instance, wierd rock formations at dusk etc)

6 Encourage pupils to observe for themselves the developments of the four seasons, and keep a nature diary which might include such things as
weather patterns   wild flowers
plant and tree growth/leaf colours   nesting activities
farming activity   birds and butterflies observed

See also
Other Worlds
Noticing
Curiosity
The Amazing World of Mankind
Seeing

OTHER WORLDS

Focus

To stimulate pupils' curiosity in relation to the natural environment.

For reflection

If you met a Martian, what questions would you want to ask?

There are obvious ones like:

> 'How did you get here?'

and typically 'British' questions like:

> 'What was the weather like on Mars when you left?'
>
> 'Would you like a cup of tea?'

and 'Please can I have a ride on your flying saucer?'

but no doubt you would think of many other questions that might encourage the Martian to tell you more about Mars and about Martians.

As human beings, we want to know about other planets, and especially we want to know whether there are other people out there somewhere. Huge rockets, with spacecraft carrying cosmonauts, cameras and expensive equipment, are sent on journeys into space so that we can find out more than we know at present. It's all very exciting, and very expensive.

But there are many other 'worlds' around us that can be visited at no cost whatsoever. For example, there is a 'world' that exists in the nature pond, and there is a different 'world' in the rock pool on the seashore. There is an ant 'world', in which the workers seem to be forever hurrying along in single file, carrying nothing as they travel in one direction, and then returning with loads sometimes bigger than the ants themselves. There is a world of bees and a world of wasps and, if you move a large stone or a flower pot in the garden, it is likely that you will uncover a world of woodlice or slugs.

Then, too, there are the worlds of animals such as rabbits, badgers and foxes. Can you imagine what life might be like inside a rabbit warren?

Imagine that, rather like Alice in Wonderland, you shrink in size – but you become much smaller than Alice. So small, in fact, that you are no bigger than a mouse. Now, if you met a mouse, what questions might you ask?

'Do you have many brothers and sisters?'

'Please, can I have a peep into your home?'

'What food do you enjoy, besides cheese?'

'What do you do during the daytime – where do you go?'

'Do you have any friends among the other animals?'

'Who are your enemies? Who don't you like?'

and so on. Think of as many questions as you can.

Or perhaps you would rather put questions to an ant, or a rabbit, or a tadpole or some other creature. One interesting question to ask would be,

'What do you think about human beings? Do they frighten you, or do they treat you kindly?'

If only we could talk with the animals, just think how much we could learn about them, and they about us. In the musical *Dr Doolittle* the doctor shares a similar thought:

> Think what it would mean
> If I could talk to the animals.
> Just imagine it,
> Chatting to the chimp in chimpanzee.
> Imagine talking to a tiger,
> Chatting to a cheetah
> What a neat achievement it would be.
>
> If I could talk to the animals,
> Learn their languages, maybe take an animal degree,
> I'd study elephant and eagle, buffalo and beagle,
> Alligator, guineapig and flea.

I'd learn to converse in polar bear and python,
And I would curse in fluent kangaroo.
If people asked me,
'Can you speak rhinocerus?'
I'd say, 'Of courseros! –
Can't you?'

I'd confer with our furry friends,
Man to animal, think of the amazing repartee.
If I could walk with the animals,
Talk with the animals,
Grunt and squeak and squawk with the animals,
And they could talk to me.

Leslie Bricusse

At first we might think that the planets and the worlds of the ants and the rabbits and the tadpoles have nothing in common. But is that really so? The fact is, we all – ants, rabbits, tadpoles and so on – live in our own little worlds within one big universe. It would be just as impossible for you or me to become a Martian (if there were such a person) as to become an ant or a rabbit or a tadpole. And it would be just as difficult for a Martian or an ant or a rabbit or a tadpole to become human.

Each of these worlds is quite amazing in its own way, and how they came to be so different is a very difficult question to answer. One thing is certain, as human beings *we have a responsibility to respect, and to protect equally, our own world and the worlds of others.*

Things to do

1 Working in small groups, ask pupils to compile a list of questions designed to find out more about the life, living conditions and life style of a bird, animal (other than domestic), fish, insect, or any other creature of the group's choosing.

   Compare responses in whole class/group discussion.

2 Working either individually or in pairs, ask pupils to write 'a day from the diary of ... (a choice made from the list given above).

   Although the diary entry will be imaginary, it should be informed by thorough research and based on factual knowledge and information.

   Finished pieces should be shared and, possibly, displayed.

3 Ask pupils to find out all they can about endangered species. If pictures are available they should be assembled and arranged to form a whole class/group collage, and notes should be added describing the nature of the threat to the species chosen.

4 Working either individually or in pairs, ask pupils to design a travel agent's advertisement encouraging people to visit another planet. Pupils should be allowed to choose their own planet, but should carry out enough research to provide the prospective traveller with the sort of information he or she would want. For example:

How far away is it?

How long will it take to get there and back?

What is there to see?

What are the conditions like?

and so on.

5 Ask pupils to answer individually, either orally or in writing, the following questions:

'If you were not human, which of the various other 'worlds' do you think you would like to belong to? What are your reasons?'

See also

The Wonderful World of Nature

Curiosity

Noticing

The Amazing World of Mankind

RULES AND COMMANDMENTS

Focus

To examine rules of different sorts;

To encourage pupils to create their own 'ten commandments'.

For reflection

'You must obey the rules!'

But what is a rule?

Usually we think of a rule as an instruction that has to be obeyed, or else ... Or else, what?

Well that depends, because rules seem to come in different shapes and sizes. For example:
- There are the laws of the country, and if we break those laws we could be made to pay a fine or, in particularly serious cases, we could be sent to prison;
- There are rules for games, such as ball games of various kinds, and other sports activities;
- There are rules that tell us what we have to do if we want to enter a competition;
- There are school rules;
- There are rules at home;
- Even among a gang of friends there is sometimes a natural leader who makes the rules and decisions that others follow.

But *why* do we need rules? Indeed, *do* we need rules?

Perhaps the easiest way to answer the question is to imagine what things would be like without rules. For example, imagine trying to cross the street in a busy town at rush hour if there were no traffic laws. Imagine if there were no laws to protect honest people against thugs and burglars. Clearly we need laws, and we need people like policemen to make sure the laws are obeyed.

And can you imagine a football match being played without rules?

What about school rules – why do we have them? What would life be like at school without any rules?

Even at home there are rules. They may not be written down, but usually there is a clear understanding about what can and cannot be done, and about what sort of behaviour is expected, and so on.

The fact is, that wherever people live, work or play together, it is almost always helpful to have a few rules which, when they are followed, will help those people to be together without misunderstanding.

This has always been so. It is more than 3000 years since the Ten Commandments in the Old Testament of the Bible were engraved on tablets of stone. The Commandments told the Israelites what they must not do – they must not commit murder, they must not steal, they must not lie, and so on. But the need for rules and laws is just as great today as it was 3000 years ago.

Some rules – like the *you must not* rules of the Ten Commandments – make quite clear what is right and what is wrong. If we disobey the laws of our country (or any other country for that matter), that is wrong and we will be punished. These rules and laws seem to teach us what is right by telling us what will happen to us if we don't do as they say!

There are other rules – like school rules and 'rules' in the home – that are there to guide rather than to force. They are intended to make life better and smoother for everyone. Although punishment may have to be used from time to time when those rules are broken, it is important to understand why they were made.

But the most effective rules, laws, or commandments are the ones we make for ourselves. We know what is right and what is wrong. We know our own strengths and weaknesses. We know the sort of things that can tempt us to behave in a way that lets us down.

With all this knowledge we have about ourselves, let us each create our own, personal Ten Commandments. But let us make one important change compared with the original Commandments. Instead of saying what we must not do, let's begin each commandment with '*I must ...*'

Then, of course, we have to make sure that we live by the the standards we have set ourselves. *We must obey the rules!*

Things to do

1 Jacqueline Brown's poem 'The Seven Commandments According to Mum' takes a light-hearted look at one mum's rules of the home. But the commandments are worth examining more closely. Beyond mum's

sergeant-major-like commands, there is a caring attitude and an expected code of behaviour that, she believes, will help her child to become a respectful and responsible person. Her rules, however unpopular, have a purpose.

The Seven Commandments According to Mum

You must   Eat fish.
                   It's good for you.
                   I don't care if the bones could throttle you
                   and it looks like the eyes are still in.
                   You can always leave the skin.

You must   Wash your ears and neck.
                   Potatoes grow in muck.
                   I don't care if the soapy water runs off
                   your elbows and soaks your vest.
                   What do you mean – being nude is rude?

You must   Say 'Thank you
                   for having me ... for the present'.
                   I don't care if you hate it at Darren's
                   and bright red jumpers aren't the In thing.
                   At your age you shouldn't be following fashion.

You must   Walk the dog.
                   It's your job.
                   I don't care if it's raining cats as well
                   and your wellies make your socks go to sleep.
                   I don't care if you haven't had your dinner yet.
                   You were the one who wanted a pet.

You must   Be nicer to your sister.
                   She's younger than you.
                   I don't care if she borrowed your bike
                   without asking and poisoned your goldfish.

| | I don't care if she did dent your bumper.
| | You must not thump her.
| You must | Honour your parents.
| | They're your Mum and Dad.
| | I don't care if you wish we'd never had you.
| | I don't care if Shaun answers back all the time.
| | That's his mother's problem. You're mine.
| You must | Go to bed.
| | You've to be up in the morning.
| | I don't care whether it was sighing or yawning.
| | Don't be daft – upstairs isn't cold.
| | I couldn't care less what programme's still on.
| | You must do as you're told.

2 As we go about our daily lives, we frequently meet signs telling us where we can't go, or what we must do. Signs such as 'Keep off the grass', 'No Entry', 'Staff only', 'Slow Children Crossing' etc. But many road signs convey their meaning without using words. Signs indicating danger ahead, sharp bend, falling rocks, etc. Pupils will give examples.

Ask pupils to design signs, without words, that might be used around the school to encourage thoughtful behaviour, and to help make the school a pleasant and well-cared for environment.

A few suitable 'topics' (there are many others) might include:
- Please place litter in the waste bin
- Please wipe your feet
- Visitors, this way please
- Wear safety goggles
- Please place bags where no-one will trip over them
- Be cheerful and friendly
- Queue here in single file
- Please keep the room tidy
- Walk quietly along the corridor
- Please return your dirty plates here

3 '*I must ...*': Ask pupils to write their own, personal Ten Commandments, each beginning with '*I must ...*'. As far as possible create an opportunity and atmosphere in which pupils can reflect on their needs, so that the completed commandments *have meaning for them*. Since these are private commandments, some pupils may prefer not to share all, or any, of their thoughts with others.

For pupils who need a few suggestions to get them started, the following may help:
– They should consider their behaviour or attitude
- towards their parents/brother/sister;
- towards their friends;
- towards those they don't like or get on with;
- towards strangers;
- towards those less fortunate than themselves;
- towards the environment;
- towards things that belong to other people.

They should consider personal qualities, such as
- their moods;
- their honesty/trustworthiness;
- their attitude towards their work.

See also

Freedom

I Wish

Honesty

Trust

LIFE IS NOT A VIDEO RECORDER!

Focus

To focus on today, while learning from the past and planning for the future.

For reflection

If you were a real life video recorder and you could press your rewind button for an action replay, what moments or scenes from your *past* would you like to live through again?

Can you remember any occasions when you were especially happy? Why was that? What caused your happiness?

Can you remember something you did at school that you were pleased with – either in the classroom or in a games lesson or, perhaps, in a concert/play or some other activity?

Can you remember something you did out of school that you were pleased with? Perhaps you achieved success in something, or did something that was particularly helpful to someone else.

But, while there are things you would like to remember, no doubt there are other things you would you like to rub out!

Was there something that happened that you wish had not happened? Was there something you said to, or about, someone that was hurtful or untrue?

Was there something you did that was wrong or unkind?

Now press your fast forward button.

How do you see yourself in the *future*? Try to imagine yourself in 10 years time.

Have you left school?

Are you still studying – perhaps at college or university?

What do you enjoy doing? What are you good at?

Now, try to imagine yourself in 20 years time.

What is your job?

Where are you living? Have you, perhaps, moved to another part of the country, or even to another part of the world?

Who are the important people in your life?

But you're not a video recorder, and you can never completely erase what happened in the past. Nor can you leap into the future. The one bit of your life that you can really do something about is what is happening *now* – what is happening today.

So, what can you do *today* that will be a step towards making the visions you had of yourself in 10 years time and 20 years time come true? Remember, by then today will be in the past, and you will not be able to wind back to re-record!

Things to do

1 Ask pupils, working individually, to list 10 memories from their past that they will never forget and would like to replay. The memories can relate to anything – successes, particularly happy occasions, things that happened in school or out of school, occasions when the pupil made someone else happy or helped them to achieve something.

Allow time for sharing, either in small groups or as a whole class/group.

2 Ask pupils, working individually, to imagine themselves in 30 years time as the subject of a *This is Your Life* type programme. It is not important for them to be famous but, hopefully, they will be interesting characters.

What sort of life would they hope to be leading? Where?

Who would be the important people around them?

What sort of things would they hope to have achieved by then?

What might they still have planned for the future?

If one of the pupil's present teachers was interviewed, how might that teacher describe the pupil?

How would the pupil like to be seen in the eyes of others? What personal qualities would he or she hope they would be able to praise?

3 '*Building bricks*': The purpose of this activity is to demonstrate that just as imposing buildings are often constructed from individual bricks or stones, so long-term ambitions and personal goals are reached through small, everyday achievements.

To illustrate and record the fact graphically, each pupil should be provided with an outlined brick wall, such as the one below (although, obviously, many variations are possible):

Each day pupils are asked to set themselves one *achievable* target in relation to:
a something they want to achieve or some difficulty they want to overcome in their school work;
b something they want to achieve out of class, e.g. succeeding or improving in some activity; completing a task that needs doing.

At the end of the day the pupil should *honestly* decide whether the targets have been achieved.

Each target equals one brick in the wall.

A third brick should relate to the pupil's relationship with others, e.g. being cheerful and friendly; helping others; behaving well; showing responsibility, and being able to get on without fuss.

It is not always appropriate to plan ahead for this aspect but, looking back, pupils usually know how successful they have been.

(Remember the activity is designed to focus on self-awareness rather than on absolute standards. Nothing will be gained by pupils cheating themselves.)

It is suggested that a colour code is used for each of the aspects. For example, blue might be used to indicate that an in-class target has been achieved, red for an out-of-class achievement, and green for relationships. Three bricks should be allocated to each day and the date should be entered. If a target has not been reached the brick should remain uncoloured. After a short while strengths and weaknesses may begin to emerge. Too many blank bricks will obviously undermine the strength of the whole wall.

It is very important for this activity to be used *positively*. Careful attention should be given to *appropriate individual* target setting to *enable pupils to taste success*. Frequent teacher support and monitoring is essential. Pupils need moral support and need their efforts to be recognised.

If the suggestion of 'each day' is too demanding, be prepared to extend the period to two or three days, but *always* fix a deadline and never allow more than one week to elapse. To use larger time blocks would destroy the purpose of the task

See also

Good Times and Bad Times

I Wish

Rules and Commandments

GOOD TIMES AND BAD TIMES

Focus

To help pupils use past experiences to influence future behaviour.

For reflection

That was cool! That was great! That was brilliant!

Three expressions – the sort we use when we are particularly pleased or excited with something that has happened.

Think of something that has happened in the last few days that might be described as cool or great or brilliant. What was the *best* thing that happened? Try to recall how you felt.

What made you feel good?

What did you do about the way you felt? Did you tell someone?

Was what happened a surprise?

Was it somewhere you went?

Was it something you received – a present perhaps?

Was it something you did, something you achieved?

Was it something you said?

Did it involve someone else?

Was it something someone else did or said?

Just what was it that pleased you?

Now think of some less pleasant happening that occurred to you recently. Something that happened that you didn't enjoy.

How did it come about?

Did it involve someone else?

Do you still feel saddened by what happened?

Was it a disappointment? Something you had hoped for but didn't happen?

Have you discussed what happened with anyone?

Was there anything you could have done to have prevented it from happening? Think carefully and be honest with yourself.

What can you *learn* from these experiences?

We often say that things happen *to* us – almost as if we have no control over what happens in our lives. Occasionally things do happen that we can do nothing about – such as an illness that prevents us from going to a party we've looked forward to for weeks, or an accident that *really was* someone else's fault!

But most times we *cause* things to happen by our own behaviour.

If we're not cheerful and pleasant with other people, we shouldn't be surprised if we find ourselves short of friends.

If we don't willingly do things for others, we can scarcely expect them to do things for us.

If we don't genuinely thank people for what they do for us, or for presents they give us, we can't complain when they begin to show more interest in others.

If we don't try as hard as we should, whether in school work, games or anything else, we can only blame ourselves when the result is disappointing.

Most times we cause things to happen by what we say or don't say, by the appreciation or lack of appreciation we show to other people, or by the effort or lack of effort we put into making a success of whatever we're doing.

Think again about the two experiences you chose. Did those things happen *to* you – or did they happen partly *because* of you?

Things to do

1 The *For reflection* passage focuses pupils' thoughts particularly on *how they felt* about pleasant and not so pleasant incidents in their lives. But for pupils to learn from an experience it is necessary to strip away the feeling response in order to examine the *factual* sequence of events that ultimately led to that response.

This activity uses role play and should be demonstrated by the teacher and a pupil.

The teacher assumes the role of a friendly policeman investigating an incident. The incident to be investigated is some less pleasant happening that occurred recently, and the pupil is the prime witness.

[The teacher should consult with the pupil before the activity begins to ensure that the experience to be investigated is 'safe' – i.e. that it does not have the potential for leading into areas that could be problematic].

The policeman interrogates the witness to discover the facts – the history of the case from its beginnings to the outcome. Information must be gathered by asking questions, not by suggesting answers or seeming to take sides. The policeman cannot accept as evidence the witness's feelings or interpretations. Nor is this the right time for the witness to defend his or her actions, decisions or behaviour.

Once the factual evidence has been collected, two or three other pupils can become involved as a 'jury' to examine the facts *neutrally and sensitively*. The function of the jury is *not to attribute blame* and responsibility. Its task is to identify any point in the evidence where a choice of actions/decisions was possible and, if appropriate, to involve the witness in discussing alternatives.

The witness *must not feel threatened*. The emphasis should be on *what* happened, *not* on *who* was responsible.

When the teacher demonstration has been concluded and understood, the process can be repeated by pupils working in small groups. It is important for every witness to be a volunteer, and for the incident to be approved by the teacher.

The aim is to train pupils in the difficult task of examining their attitudes and behaviour objectively, and the activity can obviously be used in a wide range of circumstances.

2 Ask pupils, working individually, to make two lists: one of good things and one of less pleasant things that have happened in the past – not necessarily just in the last few days.

Then remind them (preferably with examples) of the last two paragraphs of the *For reflection* passage, and repeat the final question: 'Did these things happen *to* you – or did they happen partly *because* of you?

Ask pupils to consider carefully each item on their lists and place against each either a *T* for 'to' (something that happened *to* them), or *B* for *because*.

3 Ask pupils, working individually, to list words or phrases they like to hear said to them or said about them. The activity can then be opened up for sharing and whole class/group discussion, using appropriate pauses for reflection.

How do they feel when they hear these words?

Do they feel good? Do they feel appreciated?

Do they feel that they want to do more, or try harder, for the person who is paying the compliment?

Do they feel brighter and more lively in themselves?

How often do the pupils use similar words of praise and encouragement to others?

How do those other people feel and respond?

How do the pupils feel?

'Kind words cost so little, yet mean so much! Why don't we use them more often?'

Pupils might like to copy this thought and place it in a prominent position – perhaps in the bedroom.

See also

Happiness

Sadness

Radiators and Drains

Life is Not a Video Recorder

IS THERE ANY BODY THERE?

Focus

To raise pupils' awareness of their own body.

For reflection

How well do you know your body?

How well do you know your hands, your feet, your fingers, your toes, your eyes, your nose, and so on?

For example, what is your right hand doing at this moment? How does it feel? Is it open? Is it closed? Is it relaxed? Are the fingers bent or straight? Precisely what is it doing?

And what is that beneath your left foot? Ah! So you can move your left foot! How did you move it? Which muscles did you move? Did your ankle or knee joint bend? Did your toes give a slight wiggle to re-adjust their position as you moved your foot?

Let us try an experiment:

Close your eyes. Place your hands in front of you, about twenty centimetres from your chest, and facing each other but not touching. Imagine, with all your concentration, that you are holding a balloon between them. Still holding that balloon, slowly turn your hands so that one hand is now below the balloon and the other is above. Be aware of how your hands and arms are moving, and notice the movement in your upper arms above the elbows. Now imagine that the balloon is getting heavier, but you have to keep it at the same height. It is getting gradually heavier, and heavier still … and has now become as solid and as heavy as a rock.

Have you noticed any change in the muscles in your forearms? It is quite probable that they tightened at the suggestion that the weight between your hands was getting much heavier. Open your eyes.

In fact, we mostly don't even notice how our limbs perform the tasks we ask of them. We say run, and they run for us. They climb, they pick things up – and all without us having to stop and think about what is happening. It is only when things go wrong that we really take notice – as, for example, when we are unable to use our writing hand, and have to struggle to comb our hair or lift a cup to our lips using the other hand. Then we have to concentrate much harder on how things are done.

Occasionally we listen to our bodies when they tell us there is a need to eat, or drink, or sleep, or there is a need for more clothes because it is getting cold. But, generally, we just don't give them enough attention unless we want to improve our appearance or increase our strength to impress someone else!

Just imagine yourself standing before a full length mirror. If your body could speak to you, what do you think it would say?

Would it feel that it is well-exercised and cleaned?

Would it feel that it is given a healthy diet, and not too much junk food?

Would it feel that it could do a lot more, if only you would encourage it?

Some people really do realise not only *what their bodies need*, but also *what their bodies can achieve*, and they work hard to acquire skills, sometimes in athletic and sporting activities (where they might become highly skilled athletes, or footballers, or ballet dancers), but often also in occupations requiring delicate touch and precise control (such as concert pianists, surgeons and watchmakers). No doubt you can think of other examples where people train their bodies to perform highly skilled tasks or activities.

Then, too, there are some who are admired because of their muscular physique or the shape of their body. Because of the quality of their skin, or the beauty of their hair. And there are those who train their eyes to see what most people miss (like policemen or artists, for example); those who hear what few others hear (such as skilled birdwatchers), and those who can recognise the quality of a product – such as coffee, fruit or wine – by its smell.

Whatever we would like our bodies to achieve, one thing is certain, we have to begin by *being aware of what is happening now*. Think of yourself as sitting at a large control desk, from which you are able to tune in to any part of your body, at any time, to discover what is happening – to check on how well it is performing. Pay close attention to what you find, and be honest. You will probably find areas that are often neglected or ill-treated (such as feet, nails and teeth), some that need more exercise, and some that could achieve a lot more with a little disciplined support from you. Once you have the information, then you can decide in what ways you can help your body to perform better.

How well do your know your body?

At present the answer is probably, 'Not very well!' but no doubt things will improve a good deal in the near future.

Things to do

1 The most natural activity of all is breathing, and it is probably the one we are least conscious of. This activity is intended to help pupils become aware of their breathing.

    Ask pupils to sit with their backs straight and shoulders back but not strained. The head should be upright with the eyes looking slightly downwards, and the fingers should be clasped together lightly in the lap.

    While in this position, ask pupils to close their eyes to cut out any distraction.

    Explain to pupils that as they perform this exercise you want them to breathe through their nostrils, and you want them to feel cool air entering the nostrils and warm air leaving. The length of the breaths will increase from a count of one in and one out, to a count of six in and six out. You will count quietly for them. There must be no other noise.

IN: One	OUT: One
IN: One, two	OUT: One, two
IN: One, two, three	OUT: One, two, three

    and so on, until

    IN: One, two, three …six   OUT: One, two, three …six

    Repeat the exercise to ensure that pupils are familiar with the process, and on the completion of the second cycle, ask pupils to continue breathing deeply to a pattern with which they are comfortable. After a short while ask pupils to open their eyes.

    Explain to them that deep breathing is frequently used to reduce feelings of nervousness, fear, stress, and anger (See: 'Fear', 'Anger' *Things to do*).

2 *Deep relaxation*: An effective way of raising pupils' awareness of their bodies is to lead them through a deep relaxation exercise. Ideally pupils should be lying on their backs in a relaxed state, but should this not be possible because of lack of space or other circumstances, the seated posture described above is an appropriate alternative. Remind pupils that, except for your voice giving instructions, there must be silence throughout. As before, ask pupils to close their eyes to avoid distractions, and to begin by taking two or three deep breaths.

Now ask pupils to focus on their hands. Ask them to clench their fists, and be aware of the tightened muscles. Ask them to hold this position for ten seconds and, when you tell them, to relax their hands totally, feeling the tension drain from the muscles.

Now ask them to bend their arms, clench their fists, and tighten their biceps.

As before, they are to hold that position until told to relax (after ten seconds), when they will again feel the tension drain from their muscles.

Tell them to raise both arms in front of them, and to be aware of the weight of the arms. Hold (for ten seconds) and then relax.

Move the attention to the feet, and ask the pupils to tighten the feet by curling their toes. Hold ... and relax.

Ask them to point their toes up, to tighten the calf muscles. Hold ... and relax.

If they are in a lying position, ask them to tighten their knees ... and relax.

Continue by asking pupils to tighten, hold (for ten seconds) and then relax:
    the stomach muscles
    the chest
    the shoulders
    the jaw
    the cheeks, by holding a tight smile
    the forehead, by puckering the brow into a frown.

Finally, ask pupils to tighten the whole body ... and relax.

They should remain totally relaxed for 30 seconds if sitting, or for as long as seems appropriate if pupils are lying in a relaxed state. It is helpful to bring pupils out of deep relaxation by counting, aloud, downwards from ten.

3 Ask pupils, without deliberately changing their behaviour, to become aware of the movements of their mouths, for a period of 5–10 minutes.

They will discover that a mouth does much more than eat, drink and kiss!

In particular, the movement of the mouth often provides a clue to what a person is thinking or feeling.

If pupils find the self-awareness aspect difficult, they might first observe another pupil – preferably from a distance, in order not to disturb and distract that person's natural behaviour pattern.

4 Working either in small groups or as a whole class/group, ask pupils to assume the following roles:
   a A tennis player at the point of serving;
   b A robot;
   c A nun, walking among the cloisters of an abbey;
   d A young gymnast, walking along a bar;
   e A window cleaner, cleaning a large plate glass window;
   f An elderly, blind person crossing the road;
   g A mannequin, modelling an evening gown;
   h A jockey, riding the favourite, approaching the winning post;
   i Someone scrubbing a floor;
   j A furniture remover (possibly with the assistance of a partner).

The purpose of this activity is to raise pupils' awareness of the specific adjustments they have to make to their normal movements in order to achieve their new role. This point is often more fully appreciated if the activity is frozen at an appropriate moment. Ask pupils which muscles, point of balance, angle of posture etc., they regard as being most important to the interpretation of a particular role.

See also

Body Language

Touch

Fear

Anger

TOUCH

Focus
To raise awareness of our use of touch to increase our understanding of the world around us.

For reflection
Are you a *touching* person? Or, to use the correct word, are you a *tactile* person – are you someone who enjoys touching things?
What sort of things do you especially like to touch?
- Things that are soft and furry – such as the coat of a pet dog or cat?
- Things that are soft and smooth – like silk?
- Things that are smooth and hard and shiny – like a marble surface, or a piece of sculpture?
- Do you like the feeling of dry sand trickling between your toes on a warm, sunny beach?
- Do you like to get between freshly washed sheets when you have just taken a bath?

What are your favourite 'touching' sensations? Are there things you can't help touching – things you find difficult to resist?

Are there things you wouldn't want to touch, or feel you couldn't touch? For example, some people feel unable to touch snakes, or snails, or fish, or frogs, or maggots, or spiders and insects. Why do you think this is so?

Have you ever been surprised – pleasantly or unpleasantly – when you have touched something for the first time?

How we touch something depends upon what it is, and why we are touching it. We might *stroke* something that is smooth, but what sort of things might
- we *squeeze*,
- or *pat*,
- or *pinch*,
- or *dip into*,
- or *poke*,
- or *scratch*?

Can you think of other ways of touching?

Do we learn something different about a thing depending on how we touch it?

How are the touching *sensations* different from each other?

Of course, sometimes we are the ones being touched rather than doing the touching. For example, we can be touched by the weather. In spring strong March winds blow through our hair. In summer, when we are on holiday, we can feel the heat of the sun, and the contrasting cold of waves breaking against our legs and spraying our bodies. In autumn and winter, we feel rain drops or snowflakes on our faces, and perhaps frost nipping painfully at our ears and fingers.

And we are often touched by other people. Have you ever been comforted by being hugged when you were feeling unwell or hurt? Have you ever enjoyed being tickled?

Sometimes we are touched by pet animals. Have you ever been licked by a dog and also by a cat? Was there a difference?

Why is touching so important to us?

It is important, partly because it can be very enjoyable, but particularly because it is often the best way to find out what we want to know. By touching we can find out whether a thing is hot or cold, rough or smooth, wet or dry, light or heavy. And we don't always use our fingers to get the information we want. Sometimes we use our toes – as when we are finding out how warm the water is in a swimming pool or the sea. The cheek is frequently used to test whether washing is sufficiently dry and aired, and the temperature of milk to be given to a baby is often checked against the tender skin on the underside of the mother's elbow.

We probably give less thought to touch than to any of the other senses. We all think from time to time what it must be like to be blind or deaf, but we seldom think what it would be like to lose the sense of touch. Sadly, anyone who has been paralysed as the result of an accident knows only too well.

But most of us fail to realise how important our touch is to us. Our sensitive skin is constantly sending messages to the brain – messages that enable the brain to help us make sense of the environment and the world we live in – and we can assist that process. Just as we can improve our seeing and improve our listening so, too, we can improve our touching *by being aware of the sensations* when we touch a thing, rather than just doing so automatically, without thinking.

As an experiment, close your eyes and, using your right hand, very, very lightly and gently stroke the back of your left hand. Repeat the stroking three or four times. As you do so, notice first the sensation in the back of the left hand ... and then the sensation in the fingers of the right hand.

Notice how very different the feelings are .... You can open your eyes.

Maybe that little experiment has proved a point. When next you touch, whatever you touch, be aware of the nature of the sensation. You could well become a very tactile person!

Things to do

1 Working in small groups and then as a whole class/group, ask pupils to discuss their favourite 'touching' sensations – the things they find difficult to resist.

 Encourage them to describe each sensation, as if explaining it to someone who has never had that experience. Of course, such sensations are often very difficult describe and can best be attempted by likening the experience to something else.

 The accuracy of the description is of limited importance. The purpose of the task is to raise pupils' awareness of the *nature and quality* of the touching sensation.

2 Working as for the previous task, ask pupils to suggest circumstances when it might be appropriate (a) to squeeze, (b) to pat, (c) to pinch, (d) to dip into, (e) to poke, or (f) to scratch.

 Are there other ways of touching?

 Do we learn something different about a thing depending on how we touch it?

3 The hand-stroking experiment included in the main passage can be usefully extended by pupils stroking not their own hand but the hand of a partner. With only one point of contact to focus on, awareness of the sensation is heightened.

 If the roles are then reversed, the difference in sensation between being the giver and the receiver can be appreciated.

4 Ask pupils to close their eyes. Touch each pupil lightly on the arm, back of the hand, face, or legs, with an item selected from a group of objects chosen for their contrasting tactile qualities (e.g. a feather, a shoelace, a piece of cellotape, a pan scrubber, the back of a spoon, a damp sponge/cloth, a strip of silk, the bristles side of a brush).

Ask the pupil to *say* where he/she was touched, to describe the nature of the sensation, and then identify what was used to touch them.

5 Place an 'unseen' object in a bag and ask a pupil to describe the object for the rest of the group, using only the information available to him or her through exploring the object by touch. The description should include comments on shape, texture, size, weight etc., but no hint should be given regarding its possible use. The aim is to make the description sufficiently clear to allow other pupils to identify the object.

Obviously the activity can be repeated as many times as you wish, using different objects.

6 Using images cut out from colour supplements and magazines, construct a whole class/group collage entitled 'Things we like to touch'.

See also

Is There Any Body There?

Seeing

Noticing

Silence and Sound

THINKING

Focus

To raise pupils' awareness of how they think.

For reflection

Have you ever thought what happens when you think? For instance, do you realise that you talk to yourself? Have you noticed that there often seems to be a conversation going on in your head when you need to make a decision, even over quite simple things? It might go something like this:

1st Voice	'I don't think I'll go to choir practice at lunchtime today.'
2nd Voice	'Now come on, you know you should. If you belong to something you have a responsibility to attend regularly.'
1st Voice	'But I'd rather be outside playing.'
2nd Voice	'And what would happen if everyone took the same attitude? You're just being lazy aren't you? And what about Miss Smith? How would you feel if you gave up your free time to organise things for people, and then they couldn't be bothered to turn up?'
1st Voice	'OK! I know you're right. I'll go.'

Of course, not all of the words will be 'spoken', even in our minds, but the idea of two or more different 'voices' arguing with each other is an experience we all know very well.

If you have a younger brother or sister, you will probably have seen and heard him or her actually speaking aloud to an imaginary character while playing with toys. And it is possible that you can remember when you used to talk to your imaginary friend, and perhaps even blamed your friend when you did something you knew was wrong!

But that is in the past. What sort of things do you think about now? What sort of conversations take place in your mind?

The most obvious thinking we do occurs when we have a problem to solve. Whether it is a problem in class, or for homework. or even in a practical activity such as playing a game or mending a puncture, we quickly consider and discuss in our minds what the problem is, what are the possible ways of solving it, and which of these ways we will try first. And a similar sort of conversation goes on in our heads whenever we have a choice to make.

But we also have a conversation in our heads about how we feel. We discuss in our minds and, as a result of that discussion, *we decide* whether we feel pleased, whether we feel satisfied, whether we feel that no-one cares about us, or whether we feel bored. Almost always, *how* we feel is not something that happens *to* us, it is a way *we choose to feel* because of the discussion that has taken place in our minds.

If, when we leave the house in the morning, we decide we are going to be happy, it is likely that we will be happy, and it is also likely that other people will behave cheerfully in response. But if we decide we are going to be argumentative, then obviously the day will be very different, both for us and for those who come into contact with us. Almost always, we choose how we feel.

Sometimes we think about ourselves, and discuss in our heads how good we are at something. 'I'm good at writing, but I'm not very good at sums.' You know, that sort of thinking. And sometimes we're not fair to ourselves – we can actually do better than we give ourselves credit for.

We think (perhaps too often) about what other people think about us, and we decide (perhaps too quickly) what we think about other people.

In fact, we spend a lot of time talking to ourselves – maybe not talking aloud, but nevertheless talking and discussing in our heads. Sometimes we even drift into day-dreaming – another form of talking to ourselves – when we should be concentrating on something else, such as reading, or listening to what someone is saying.

Do you think people can tell when you are thinking?

Can you tell when someone else is thinking?

Has anyone, such as a teacher or your parents, ever interrupted your day-dreaming and asked you what you were thinking?

Do you generally keep your thoughts to yourself, or do you 'say what you think'? Is there a right time for keeping your thoughts to yourself, and a right time for saying what you think?

Do you think best when you are alone or when you are with others?

Do you think better at a particular time of day? Or in a particular place?

What sort of things influence your thinking?

Are you influenced by what other people think and say?

If you are influenced by others, are they people whose opinion you can trust?

That is, do they *really* have knowledge and experience to support what they are saying?

Quite clearly, *how* we think and *what* we think are both very important.

Thinking leads to making decisions, and the decisions we make influence what we do and how we behave.

If thinking is so important, how can we decide what is good thinking and what is not so good?

Perhaps the most effective way is to pretend to be a neutral person listening to the conversation taking place in your head – rather like listening in on someone else's telephone conversation. In this way you can recognise the ideas that are helpful and positive and have a good feel about them, and you can reject those that are weak or mean or are critical in an unhelpful way.

Try to see where the thinking is leading to – to a satisfactory outcome, or to difficulties.

There is a well known BT television advertisement that says, 'It's good to talk'. We might add, 'even to yourself', – but *do listen to what you're saying to yourself!*

Things to do

1 The main passage asks, 'Is there a right time for keeping your thoughts to yourself and a right time for saying what you think?'

   Working in small groups of five or six, ask pupils to discuss this question.

   They should be asked to consider not only what effect such a decision might have on the immediate situation, but how it might affect future relationships.

2 Show pupils how to *brainstorm* using a mind-map or spidergram.

   Divide pupils into small groups and ask them to brainstorm the question 'What makes a good friend?' Present each group with a large sheet of paper and ask them to write the word FRIEND in the centre as the focus of their thinking. Remind them that this is a brainstorming exercise, and they should record whatever comes into their heads. It is only at a later stage that ideas will be discussed in greater detail, when some will be developed and other, perhaps, will be rejected.

3 Ask pupils to keep a personal diary in which, for one day, they briefly log each occasion on which it is necessary for them to make a decision. Either at the end of the day, or at some other suitable opportunity, ask them to look back over the entries and reflect on:
- How each decision was made;
- Were alternative choices considered?
- Did anyone or anything influence the choice?
- Was it the right decision?

4 Ask pupils to keep a personal diary covering a few days – possibly a week – in which they record the *different types of thinking* they experience, e.g. occasions when they have had to make choices or decisions; significant things they have learned; thoughts about themselves and others; thoughts about their work etc. It is not necessary to include detail, but the entries *must be based on personal experience*.

On a sheet of paper, ask pupils to draw an outlined head at the centre, enclosing the word 'ME'. Pupils should then record, in abbreviated form, a selection of information from their personal diaries, in 'thought bubbles' radiating from the head.

Depending on the range and quality of work produced, it could be interesting and beneficial to produce a class or group diagram as a summary of pupils' experiences.

5 Each of the words below refers to a different way of thinking:
reasoning studying brainstorming imagining considering reflecting planning pondering dreaming concentrating

Working either individually, in small groups, or as a whole class/group, ask pupils to suggest situations in which each word might be appropriately used.

See also

Curiosity

Noticing

Points of View

I Wish

What If?

SEEING

Focus

To raise pupils' visual awareness of the world around them;

To help them appreciate the value of sight.

For reflection

'Close your eyes and wait until I tell you to open them' is an instruction we all like to hear, because it usually means that when we open our eyes we will receive a pleasant surprise.

'See for yourself!' and 'I'll believe it when I see it!' are other expressions we hear from time to time. All of these expressions draw attention to the fact that most of us rely more on seeing than we do on our other senses – that is to say, more than we do on hearing, touching, smelling and tasting. We have another saying, don't we, 'Seeing is believing'. In other words, *we trust our eyes.*

So what information do our eyes give us that we would have difficulty in obtaining in any other way?

Above all they tell us the shape of the world around us:
- where things are – how near or how far;
- how big;
- what colour;
- how we can get from one place to another;
- situations that can be dangerous;

and so on.

They also enable us to see
- sights and scenes that are beautiful;
- the people we love and like;
- our pets;
- the things that entertain and interest us, such as programmes on television, and stories or information in books.

And, of course, there are times when we see things we would rather not see – such as news items about sad or unpleasant happenings.

Can you think of any other ways in which we use our eyes to gain information and experience?

Sometimes the things we see give us so much pleasure that we want other people to enjoy the experience with us. For example, many of us take lots of holiday photographs which later remind us not only of what we did, but of how we felt at the time, and of many other things about the holiday. It's often disappointing, though not surprising, that people who were not with us at the time have difficulty in sharing our level of excitement and enjoyment.

Sharing our enjoyment of anything with someone else (a TV programme, a walk, watching a football match etc.) always seems to increase the pleasure.

With or without the help of photographs, we can often recall scenes in what we call our 'mind's eye'. For example, if you close your eyes now you can probably remember what your bedroom looks like, or perhaps you can recall some things in the room but not others. Similarly, you might be able to recall mental pictures of things that happened last year, or even two or three years ago.

But not only can we recall in our mind's eye things we have seen, we can also imagine scenes that don't exist except in our imagination. Sometimes, in art lessons, you may be asked to draw or paint an imaginary scene, and when we listen to the radio we can imagine situations and scenes described by the commentator or news reporter – although what we imagine may be very different from the real thing. We *listen for clues*, and use our imagination to provide the picture.

Sometimes, when we are in the dark, our imagination can become over-active, especially if we hear an unusual noise. We prick our ears and listen for sounds and clues to tell us what is happening around us, and we can become nervous because we cannot see.

For blind people their 'real' world is shaped by the use of their other senses. Listening and touching are particularly important, but smelling and tasting are also valuable, especially in the preparation of food. By developing these senses, and by picking up all the clues available, a blind person creates his or her own mind picture of the world around, and learns how to live and move about in that world.

Just as it is necessary for the blind person to develop and sharpen these other senses, so there is a need for those of us who are able to see to improve our seeing. How can we do that? By looking more carefully at whatever we set our eyes upon.

Close your eyes and wait until I tell you to open them. When you open them I want you to look carefully at the backs of your hands, held side by side so that the thumbs are just touching. Open your eyes now.

Look at the fingers. How would you describe them? Long and thin? Short and stubby?

Look at the nails. Are they clean? Do they need trimming?

Look at the patterns of folded skin at the knuckles.

Is the colour of the skin exactly the same across both hands, or are there different shades?

Are there any scratches, cuts, bruises or other marks?

And so on.

The purpose of this example is to show that most of us are lazy when we look at something, and perhaps we are laziest of all when we are looking at something that is very familiar to us – such as the backs of our hands. No doubt some of us have just noticed things about our hands we've not seen before!

The fact is there is a difference between looking and seeing. *Seeing is more than just looking.* We sometimes say, 'Look at this! What can you see?' To see we have to look more carefully. It might be helpful if we all adopted the motto *'Don't just look – see!'*

Things to do

1 *'Say what you see'*: The purpose of this task is to encourage pupils to look very carefully, and to describe accurately what they see, i.e. factual description and not interpretation or guesswork.

   Divide the class/group into pairs and provide a viewfinder for each pair. (For this purpose a viewfinder is a piece of card or stout paper about 15 cm square from which a central 'window', 5 cm x 4 cm, has been cut.) Holding the head still and the viewfinder steady, at about 20 cm from the face, and with one eye closed, one member of each pair should describe in detail to his or her partner exactly what can be seen within the viewfinder frame. The description should include comments on
   - the size, shape, colour and texture of component elements;
   - foreground, middle ground and background;
   - relationships between different elements in the scene, such as relative size and position.

Considerable importance should be attached to the descriptive process. The very fact that pupils have to describe encourages them to look more carefully. The partner should feel able to ask questions for clarification.

Initially, it is helpful if pupils are encouraged to choose 'pictures' in which there is a single dominant feature or object.

2 *'Can we trust our eyes?'* Although we may all look at the same thing, what we see may be different. Ensure that all pupils have comfortable access to the images.

Without any preliminary discussion, what do they see?

How many first see the young woman, and how many the old?

How many can see both images?

Look at these two pictures.

3 Colley Cibber's poem 'The Blind Boy' causes us to reflect on what it might be like to be blind, while rejecting the sentimental, pitying, good intentions of those who mean well but fail to truly understand.

The Blind Boy

O say what is that thing call'd Light,
Which I must ne'er enjoy;
What are the blessings of the Sight:
O tell your poor blind boy!

You talk of wondrous things you see;
You say the sun shines bright;
I feel him warm, but how can he
Or make it day or night?

My day or night myself I make
Whene'er I sleep or play;
And could I ever keep awake
With me 'twere always day.

With heavy sighs I often hear
You mourn my hapless woe;
But sure with patience I can bear
A loss I ne'er can know.

Then let not what I cannot have
My cheer of mind destroy:
Whilst thus I sing, I am a king,
Although a poor blind boy.

Discuss the poem, and ask pupils to think about what they would miss most if they were unable to see.

4 Working individually, ask pupils to list some of the practical things they do every day – starting when they wake and ending when they go to sleep at night.

Then ask pupils to read through the list and put a mark against those things they couldn't do, or would have difficulty in doing, if they couldn't see.

5 *'Hello! It's me!'* Ask individual pupils to close their eyes or blindfold themselves. Then point to a selection of pupils and ask each to say, in his or her normal voice, 'Hello! It's me!'

How well can the blindfolded pupil recognise his or her fellow pupils by the sound of the voice only?

6 Ask pupils to cover their ears, so that they cannot hear, for a period of two minutes.

Then ask them to uncover their ears but to blindfold themselves, so that they cannot see, for a period of two minutes.

Ask them to discuss and compare the experiences.

[For teachers wishing to develop the theme of blindness further, the Royal National Institute for the Blind produce *Finding Out About Blindness: Teachers' Pack*. The pack contains lesson plans, workcards, posters, simulation spectacles and samples of braille. It is available from RNIB Customer Services, 224 Great Portland Street, London W1N 6AA Tel: 0345 456457]

See also

Noticing

The Wonderful World of Nature

Other Worlds

Silence and Sound

Touch

NOTICING

Focus

To raise pupils' visual awareness of the world around them.

For reflection

Would you make a good detective?

Are you observant? Do you notice things?

For example, would you notice if a piece of work on display in the classroom had been moved from one wall to another?

Would you notice if your teacher changed his or her clothes during the lunchtime break?

Could you recognise the prints made by your trainers on wet sand or on a muddy path?

Can you describe the curtains in your bedroom? What colour are they? Do they have a pattern?

What is the make of the TV set you use every day?

What is the design on the reverse side of a ten pence coin?

When we *notice* something, that object – or, maybe, that person – seems to stand out from everything else around it. It attracts our attention and causes us to think about what we are seeing. Sometimes what we have noticed stays in our memory, and the information may be used on some future occasion.

This is how detectives build up evidence, isn't it?

Imagine there has been a robbery at a small post office. The postmistress rings for the police. A detective arrives and asks, 'Can you describe the man, madam? How tall was he? How would you describe his build – was he fat or thin? How old was he? What colour was he? What was he wearing? Did he have any distinguishing features, such as a beard, a tattoo, a scar, or a ring through his eyebrow?'

And so on, until, bit by bit, the detective has an impression of what the suspect might look like – based on what someone has noticed.

In this imaginary example, because something had happened that was unusual, it is likely that the lady would remember details that normally she would not have noticed. This is true for most of us. *We notice things that are unusual*, but we often overlook things that are around us every day.

There are, of course, many reasons why people notice some things and not others. For example, *we notice things we're interested in* – such as differently coloured shells or pebbles on the seashore, or flowers, or butterflies, or cars, or aeroplanes, or football stickers.

What are your interests? What sort of things might you notice that a friend might not notice?

Sometimes we notice a thing *because we are curious* about how its works, or *because something appears in an unexpected place* – such as a farm tractor passing through a busy city centre, or the headteacher wearing a red nose on Red Nose Day!

Sometimes people notice things because they possess *specialist skills* that have been trained and practised over a long period of time. Police officers and detectives are obvious examples, but there are many others, ranging from artists to people living in forest areas, who are able to recognise tracks made by animals and can say how recently the tracks have been made.

Then, too, we notice things when we *need* to – perhaps when we are searching for something we have lost, or when we need to remember landmarks so that we don't get lost when next we pass that way.

Can you recall any instance when you have noticed something that proved to be important or useful later?

The fact is, during any one day our eyes look at thousands and thousands of scenes or images, but of these thousands of images we actually notice very few indeed. As long as our eyes are open they must be pointed at something, whatever that might be, but we might not be seeing what we are looking at. If our brain is thinking about something else, it is unlikely that we will 'see' what we are looking at. We will be day-dreaming.

When we truly day-dream, not only do we not 'see', we do not 'hear' either. It is as if our brain has, for the time being, shut itself off from the outside world.

Day-dreaming is relaxing and requires little or no effort. By comparison, *seeing and noticing* are more demanding. They *require concentration* and *awareness*, and we ask ourselves questions, 'What is it? Why is it there?

How does it work?' etc. The answers feed our memories and provide experiences which help us to live our lives more effectively.

You don't have to be a detective to be an observant 'private eye'.

Things to do

1 Working in small groups, ask pupils to compile a detailed description of someone they see every day but who is not present in the room, e.g. site-supervisor/caretaker.

If possible each group should be allocated a different 'subject'. The test will be to discover whether others are able to identify the person from the description given.

2 Ask pupils, working independently, to draw or describe accurately the sign on the roadside near the school which warns drivers that they are approaching a school.

3 Ask each pupil to draw a map or diagram showing a stranger how to get from school to the pupil's home. The map/diagram should include important information such as street names, and should indicate helpful landmarks.

4 *'Kim's Game':* This is a useful activity for exercising pupils' observational skills.

Each pupil will require a pencil and paper.

Place before the pupils a tray containing a number (say fifteen or so) easily recognisable objects. Pupils attempt to memorise what articles are on the tray. The tray is then removed from sight and the pupils use the pencil and paper to record the items they can recall.

There is no fixed time for pupils to study the tray. It is better if the teacher watches the pupils and makes a decision on the basis of their reactions.

As pupils become more confident, the task can be made much more difficult by increasing the number of items, or shortening the length of time allowed, or by exchanging the positions of objects and requiring pupils to say which ones have been moved.

The game should not be seen as a competition.

5 Ask pupils to draw from memory a household object with which they are very familiar, e.g. a video handset, a computer keyboard, a vacuum cleaner, a washing machine, a table lamp, a Walkman.

Explain that the task is not designed to test their drawing skills, but how well they observe items they see and use.

When the drawings are completed, collect them and ask pupils when they go home to observe very carefully the object they have drawn.

On the next appropriate occasion, ask the pupils once more to draw the same item from memory. When they have completed the task, re-issue the original drawings so that comparisons can be made.

6 Over a given period – say, a few days, or a week – ask pupils to briefly log any occasions when they have noticed things that have attracted or interested them. In general, allow pupils a free choice in the range of things they might record. For example, people's movements and reactions might be listed as well as 'fixtures' such as unusual road signs. But there may be occasions when it is appropriate to ask pupils to look out for things which re-inforce a topic or theme being studied in class.

See also

Seeing

Curiosity

Silence and Sound

The Wonderful World of Nature

Other Worlds

PATTERNS

Focus

To raise pupils' awareness of pattern in everyday life;

To explore ways of varying patterns – including patterns of habit.

For reflection

If you happened to be walking along the street and you came to a large area of smooth, wet concrete, might you feel tempted to step on it? Of course not! Such a thought would never enter your head! But if it did – just *if*, and *if* you did step on the concrete, and *if* you were wearing trainers, it is likely that not only would you leave a footprint, you would also leave a pattern.

What do we mean by a pattern? How would you describe it?

Often when we speak of a pattern we are referring to a design in which shapes and, maybe, colours are arranged in such a way that they seem to relate to each other. When the same arrangement is used more than once we say it is a repeated pattern. Repeated patterns are used a great deal for curtains, wall papers and materials for clothes. Maybe you have created a repeat pattern – perhaps using a shape carved in lino or in potato.

In fact, we are surrounded by patterns. Look around you now. Can you see any examples of pattern?

Look carefully at the clothes you and other pupils and the teachers are wearing. Look especially at shirts and blouses and ties, and at shoes, including the bottoms of shoes.

Look around the room you are in. Look for any patterns on the walls. Look at the arrangement of window panes. Look for any panelling in the doors. Look at the ceiling, the floor, the radiators, the curtains, and so on.

These are examples of man-made patterns, but there are many examples of pattern in nature.

Can you think of examples among animals, birds and butterflies? Think of patterns used as camouflage for protection. Think of patterns and colours used by some male birds to attract a mate – the peacock, for example. Think of the beautiful patterns on the wings of butterflies.

Can you think of examples among flowers of different kinds? Think of well known flowers such as poppies, tulips, pansies and lupins.

Think of other examples in nature such as snowflakes, sea shells, spiders' webs, stars in the sky.

But patterns don't only occur in things we can *see*. We also have patterns *in time*. For example, four seasons – spring, summer, autumn and winter – make one year. And for farmers especially, each season has its own range of jobs to be completed. Then, we divide each year into smaller periods of time: into months, weeks, days, hours, minutes and seconds.

We often do the same thing on the same day each week, and we may even do the same thing at the same time each day. We establish a *pattern*.

Can you think of things that you do on the same day each week?

Can you think of things that you do at the same time each day?

Of course, some things have to be done to a regular pattern because our pattern has to fit in with other people's arrangements. Getting up in a morning and getting ready for school is an example, especially if there are others who need to leave the house around the same time.

But there are other things we do in the same way each time. '*Out of habit*' is an expression we often use. 'I always put my left shoe on first' is an example. Or 'I always sit in this seat'. Or 'I always have the same lunch, every day'. These are habits, and when they are repeated they form a pattern of the way we do things, and we often do them without even thinking what we are doing.

What habits do you have?

It's true of most repeated patterns, that after a while they lose their interest for us, and we stop thinking about them. For instance, do you notice the pattern on the curtains, or on the plates, or on anything else you see in your house every day?

But if one small feature of a repeated pattern is changed, our attention is attracted to the change and we become more interested. Let us take a simple example:

Imagine that you have in front of you a chess or draughts board. It's not a particularly exciting pattern, is it – a plain mixture of black and white squares.

But if we change just one square the whole board becomes more interesting.

For example, choose one black square, about three rows in from one of the sides – it doesn't matter which – and replace that black square with a coloured square, such as a red square. The whole board becomes more interesting, more exciting and more attractive. Even if we surrounded the changed board with fifteen other boards that were purely black and white, the eyes and the attention would constantly be drawn back to the board with the coloured square.

Habits, and other things we always do in the same way, are like most repeated patterns – they become uninteresting. But, like the chess board, things can quickly be changed.

Think about the things you *always* do in the same way, and the things around you that are always in exactly the same place. Ask yourself, 'Is there a good reason for doing things the way I do, or is it just habit? Is there another way of doing things? Should I arrange my books, toys, clothes or games differently?'

You might also need to ask, 'If I change things, will it interfere with or upset other people? If the answer is 'yes', then it is clearly sensible to discuss the possible changes with them.

Remember, changing just one square on the chess board made the whole board more exciting.

Things to do

1 Ask pupils to list regular patterns in the things they do or don't do. For example:
  - things they do at the same time every week;
  - things they do at the same time every day;
  - routines they always perform in the same order, e.g. putting on clothes;
  - choices that always bring the same results, e.g choices in relation to food, music, clothes, places to go;
  - things that are always left in the same place, for no good reason, and are never re-arranged or re-organised;
  - any other examples.

2 Now that awareness has been raised relating to patterns and habits, ask pupils to keep a personal log covering two or three days during which they try to see their behaviour and habits as a neutral observer might see them. Remind pupils that a neutral observer would note good points as well as weaknesses.

3 Some actions, once they have been learned, become *automatic* and we generally perform them without having to think what we are doing – for example, walking, riding a bicycle, eating with a knife and fork.

Although the actions are repeated regularly they are not habits, they are skills for living. If we had to think about each step we take or every movement of the knife and fork, our brains would have very little time in which to think about other things!

Ask pupils to identify other *automatic skills*.

4 Of course, there are good habits as well as bad habits. For example, the good habit of always saying 'thank you' in appreciation of something that has been given either as a gift or as help. Or the good habit of tidying up a mess without needing to be asked.

Ask pupils to make two lists; one of their good habits and one of their bad habits.

They should then examine each item in turn and consider the impact of this behaviour (good or bad) on others.

5 *The chessboard*

STAGE 1

Either demonstrate the chessboard example outlined in the main passage.

Or provide each pupils with a photocopied chessboard and a gummed paper square of the appropriate size.

STAGE 2

From all of the self-knowledge and self-awareness information pupils have accumulated during the earlier activities, ask each pupil to choose just one aspect for change (the pupil's personal 'coloured square') that would modify beneficially the pattern of his or her life.

See also

Noticing

The Wonderful World of Nature

Who Am I?

Life is Not a Video Recorder

Good Times and Bad Times

SILENCE AND SOUND

Focus

To heighten pupils' awareness of the quality of sound and the quality of silence.

For reflection

We have a saying, don't we, that, 'It was so quiet you could hear a pin drop'.

Have you ever heard a pin drop? I would guess not, unless it fell onto a hard surface such as something made from metal or glass.

But you may have noticed how silence makes even the quietest sounds seem quite loud, when they occur.

Imagine you are lying in bed at night. All is quiet and you are just about to go to sleep when, suddenly, you become aware of the ticking of a clock, or the rhythmic dripping of a tap, or the occasional rattling of a door that has not been properly fastened. Normally, you probably wouldn't notice such sounds but, in the silence of the night, they can seem very loud. What is more, they're sounds that can't be ignored. You can't pretend they're not happening.

There are many other examples, aren't there – such as the fly buzzing against the window pane, or the moth clattering around inside a lampshade. No doubt you can think of others. James Kirkup was certainly able to do so in this poem called 'The House at Night'.

The House at Night

Some stealthy spider is weaving round my bed
and mice are nibbling the curtains overhead.
Weird footsteps make the floorboards crack,
the staircase creaks, chill draughts thrill down my back
from some forgotten window out of sight -
    this is the house at night.

There's a whispering on the landing
where a creepy tropic plant is standing,
and the coatrack in the hall
lets fall a scarf – a long, soft fall:
a snake's loose coils that rapidly grow tight -
    this is the house at night.

From the distant kitchen come the notes
of dripping taps, plink-plonking secret codes
I cannot get the meaning of: a sudden
icy shudder – the refrigerator groans – a hidden
oven, cooling, ticks in rustling ember-light -
    this is the house at night.

But even stranger is my own tense breathing
as I lie here speechless looking at the ceiling
that seems to swim all round like falling snow.
I can hear my eyelids batting gently, slow -
then quick as heartbeats as I freeze with fright
at something in the mirror shining bright –
has someone left the telly on all night?
No, thank heaven, it's all right,
it's only the moon's pale, spooky light
touching my tangled sheets with chalky white -
    yes, this is the house at night.

Let us try an experiment. For just one minute, close your eyes – so that you are relying only on what you hear, sit perfectly still, and remain totally silent. Try to remember any sound you hear – however quiet or however loud the sound may be – but remain perfectly still with your eyes closed.

[After one minute]

Open your eyes. Now try to recall all the different sounds you heard.

Were the sounds natural sounds – such as birds singing, or rain beating on the window pane? Or were they made by other people – perhaps talking or calling to each other? Or were they made by something mechanical – such as traffic passing by, or the ringing of a telephone?

How would you describe them – gentle, harsh, startling, jumbled, or how?

How far away were the sounds? Were some quite near and others further away?

It is likely that, not only did you hear sounds, but you used your imagination to try to explain what might have caused them. In fact, this sort of *sound detective* work is going on all the time, but obviously it works much better when we listen more attentively – as we did during the minute of silence. *Listening* is a *doing* word – it doesn't just happen. We have to make an effort. *But hearing is more than just listening.* We often say, 'Listen! What can you hear?'

Similarly, silence is more than there just being no noise. *Silence is like a space in which we can play with our thoughts.* We can think back over things that have happened. We can think about things we're going to do, and how we're going to do them. We can think of things we should have said but didn't, and of things we intend to say, but probably won't say. And, of course, we can imagine whatever we want to imagine!

Silence is exciting because we don't know what is going to happen next.

We don't know what ideas might come into our heads. We are awake to the slightest sounds, and when we are silent we sometimes see things we've not noticed before.

In other words, when we are silent we become more aware of what we're thinking, and – because we're listening and looking more sharply – we become more aware of what is going on around us.

Can you think of places (buildings) where we are expected to be quiet so that people can be silent with their own thoughts?

Can you think of the sort of outdoor places where people might go to find quiet and silence?

Of course, most often when we want to be silent we have to find some quiet corner in our own homes, and that is not always easy. But even in just one minute, as we have seen, there is time for our ears to become alert, and our imagination to come alive.

And, who knows, if we are quiet enough, we might even hear a pin drop!

Things to do

1 Discuss with pupils their response to silence.

Do they enjoy it? Do they find it threatening?

Do they seek quiet moments? Where do they go when they want to be quiet?

What happens when they are quiet?

And so on.

2 The *For reflection* passage mentions several examples of sounds that are magnified by the surrounding silence. Ask pupils to add their own examples. It might be helpful to suggest locations, such as in a gallery or museum, in the depth of the countryside, inside a cathedral, in a waiting room (such as a dentist's waiting room), etc.

3 Repeat the sustained silence exercise outlined in the main passage.

With practice, pupils improve their listening skills and increase aural awareness.

4 Create a similar silence, but on this occasion ask pupils to recall not the sounds, but the thoughts they experienced in just one minute. They may be surprised both by the number of thoughts and by the diverse range.

5 Working in small groups of about four pupils, and using classroom percussion instruments, ask pupils to perform the following musical tasks in which sound and silence are equally important:
- Create a repeated mechanical rhythm pattern (like the working of a machine or a clock). After a while the rhythm stops abruptly, and there is silence for 3 or 4 seconds – before the rhythm splutters briefly into life – followed by a further silence – and then the pattern resumes and continues as it began, uninterrupted.
- *Echoes:*
A short rhythmic pattern (no more than 2 bars) is played *forte* on a solo instrument and, after a short pause, the exact pattern is repeated *pianissimo* as a distant echo from the other side of a mountain valley.
The echo can either be played on the same instrument, or a contrast in instrumental colour may be preferred. It is possible to extend the task as the echo reverberates around the valley, becoming fainter and fainter (but not slower!)

A different pattern should then be introduced by the lead instrument and echoed in similar fashion, etc.
- Imagine a clip from a cartoon film in which a mouse steals quietly into the classroom at night. He sees various instruments lying around and gently tries each one in turn. It is good fun. The mouse calls his friends. Each takes up an instrument and dances around the room, playing quite happily. Suddenly, the dancing is brought to a halt by the arrival of the school cat. The mice scamper away to safety. The task for pupils is to provide a musical soundtrack for the film.

See also

A Bit of Peace

Alone

Touch

Thinking

Noticing

LABELS AND STEREOTYPES

Focus

To demonstrate the danger of allowing labels to stereotype individuals.

For reflection

Baked beans!   Disabled!   Boy!

Three labels. When we hear these words, or see them written, they conjure up particular ideas in our minds.

For example, baked beans, we know, are bought in tins. They are prepared in tomato sauce, and are very enjoyable when served with chips or on toast. When we see a baked beans label, these are the thoughts that spring to mind.

And what about the labels 'disabled' and 'boy'?

Perhaps 'disabled' might suggest a person who has a physical or mental problem that prevents him or her from doing some of the things other-people can do.

And 'boy' – well, we all know that a boy is a, sort of, young man who is loud, strong and brave, who doesn't cry, who plays rough games, and can build things or take them to pieces.

But there are two problems with labels:

Firstly, they can't tell us enough. For example, the label on the baked beans tin may well list in detail what is inside (beans, tomato paste, sugar, salt, water, natural flavouring, and so on), but it can't tell us what the beans *taste* like – and, after all, the taste is the reason for us wanting to buy the beans!

Secondly, a label sometimes makes us lazy and once we have placed a person in a box in our mind, marked 'boy' or 'disabled', we often stop thinking about the boy or the disabled person *as an individual*. 'He's a miner'. 'She's a nurse'. 'He's an old age pensioner'. 'She's a blonde'. These are all labels that tell us very little about the individual people, and too often we jump to conclusions about a person because of his or her label.

Are all boys loud, strong, brave and so on, any more than all girls are weak, gentle and caring, cry when they get upset, play with dolls and dolls' houses, and like cooking and washing-up? Of course not. Each boy and each girl is a mixture of all sorts of qualities which, together, make that boy or girl an individual – a unique person who is unlike any other.

In a similar way, all disabled people are different from each other. A disabled person is an ordinary person with a particular problem. Perhaps he or she can't walk or can't see, or whatever the problem may be, but in other ways most disabled people are perfectly normal, healthy human beings and want to be treated as such – as individuals.

General descriptions, such as those we used for 'boy' and 'disabled' are known as *stereotypes*. A stereotype suggests that all people or things referred to by the same label are more or less alike. Sometimes stereotype labels are used to unkindly and unfairly poke fun at groups of people, such as 'women drivers' or 'traffic wardens'.

We also use a stereotype label to refer to people from a particular country or region – such as German, Italian, Scots or Irish – suggesting that all Germans or Italians behave in a similar way. And, of course, people from other countries have their own ideas of what an Englishman is.

One of the problems created by drunken English hooligans at football matches abroad is that they are too often seen as representing English football supporters generally. The bad behaviour of a few becomes the image suggested by the label 'English football supporter'.

So, now that you understand what is meant by labels and stereotypes, try to think of other examples for yourself.

Above all, try to *be aware* on those occasions when you are tempted to use labels, and ask yourself whether what you intend to say is true of all, or just some, of the people or things to which the label refers. If it is only true of some, then say so!

Things to do

1 Assumptions about people are often based on labels which refer to:
- their appearance (punk, snooty etc.);
- their job (housewife, vicar, refuse collector etc.);
- their age ('old', 'kid'), colour or sex (male or female);
- (as in the case of the English football supporters referred to) the behaviour, attitudes or qualities of a few, who are assumed to be representative of a much larger number – maybe a whole nation.

Working in small groups, ask pupils to find an many examples as they can of each of the above.

They should then discuss how a person's label or appearance affects the way people behave towards them. Pupils should try to find both positive and negative examples – such as labels that invite respect and approval, and labels that are associated with low status or undesirable behaviour; those who are not treated fairly because of their appearance (perhaps because of their shabby clothes, unconventional hair style, or rings in unusual places), and those whose appearance works in their favour (such as attractive and well-groomed young ladies), leading to opportunities that might not otherwise exist.

2 Labels are often very difficult to remove from old bottles. Similarly, some people earn reputations for something they have done early in their lives, and those reputations (or labels) stay with them for many years, sometimes throughout their lives.

Ask pupils, in their small groups, to discuss and give examples of:
a people who are pleased to be remembered for what they have done in the past (e.g. retired sports personalities);
b people who want their past to be forgotten, because they have changed their lives for the better (e.g. repentant criminals).

3 The same label can bring different responses from different people. For example, imagine the label 'young people' as it might be used by an old age pensioner, living alone, whose life is made miserable by the threatening behaviour of a gang of teenagers. Then, think how a youth leader might comment on young people. Thirdly, what might be said by an eleven year-old who believes that adults just don't understand young people?

Divide pupils into groups of four. One pupil will be a TV interviewer, one will be the old age pensioner, one the youth club leader, and the fourth the eleven year-old. The group should prepare interviews for performance. It will be the task of the interviewer to obtain from each of the characters their views on 'young people today'. The pupils being interviewed should attempt to become 'real' characters - thinking who they are, their name, their age, who their friends are, what they do during the day, what they watch on TV, what are their likes and dislikes etc.

The interviewer should try to develop a dialogue, and should not be content with one sentence answers.

Using a similar structure, the group should prepare performances on the labels 'old age', 'parents', and 'teachers'. In each case it will be necessary to introduce three characters with differing views.

4 Ask pupils to look for examples of labels and stereotypical descriptions in newspapers (especially in headlines designed to attract attention), and on TV (especially in advertisements, and programmes which include audience comment and opinions).

If possible, select a range of examples for wall display.

See also

Them and Us

There's No-one Quite Like You

What If? *(Things to do)*

Radiators and Drains

What Makes a Hero?

WHAT IF?

Focus

To encourage pupils to empathise with others: to view a situation from a changed perspective.

For reflection

Have you ever wished you were someone else?

Have you ever wished, perhaps, that you were a well known television personality? Or a DJ? Who do you think you might like to be?

What if you were a pop star, or a famous sportsperson, or a headteacher, or even Prime Minister?

But let's leave the 'being famous' bit until a little later in your life, and let's think, for the moment, about a few other 'What If's?'

What if you had been born a girl instead of a boy, or a boy instead of a girl?

How different would your life be?

Are there things you would be able to do that you can't do now?

Are there things you wouldn't be able to do that you can do now?

Do you think people would treat you differently?

Would life generally be better or worse?

What if you had been born in a different country? What if you had been born, say, in India, or South Africa, or Bosnia, or in the United States of America – how might your life be different?

What if you had been born with a different coloured skin? Might the colour of your skin affect the way people behave towards you?

What if you had been born at a different time – say in the Middle Ages? Or in the time of Elizabeth I instead of Elizabeth II? Or at the end of the last century instead of this?

What would you have eaten?

What would you have worn?

What medicines would have been available if you were ill?

What would school have been like?

How different would your life have been?

Is 'What If?' just a game we can play? Not necessarily. Because, if we really think what the true answers to our What If? questions might be, and if we take the trouble to gather information and find out more, then our understanding will be much greater than it was before we asked the question.

Situations occur everyday when, for us to understand why someone is behaving the way they are, we need to ask ourselves, 'What if I were that person? How would I feel? What would I think? How would I behave?'

For example:
- Imagine that, in the playground, you and your friends are playing a game but, for whatever reason, one boy or girl is not invited to join in. What if you were that boy or girl – how would you feel?
Or
- What if you were the boy or girl who is made fun of because you are always last in a race?
Or
- What if you were your mother or father whose child (you) arrived home very, very late after playing with friends? How would you feel? What would you do?

By asking 'What If?' questions we can begin to understand other people and, most importantly, it is possible we can make life more pleasant for them and for ourselves. We just have to try and answer those four key questions:

'What if I were that person? How would I feel? What would I think? How would I behave?'

Things to do

1 Divide pupils into small groups of three or four. Ask them to discuss and list the advantages and disadvantages of being:
   - a television personality;
   - a pop star;
   - a famous sportsperson;
   - Prime Minister.

Guide pupils to consider in each case the nature and *quality of everyday life* rather than just the glamour aspect and the changes in material circumstances.

2 Working in small groups (comprising both boys and girls, if possible) ask pupils to identify any ways in which the lives of boys really are very different from the lives of girls, and *vice versa* – other than the obvious fact that girls can have babies.

Would any pupil wish to have been born a girl instead of a boy, or a boy instead of a girl?

[N.B. Both of the above activities can be used and extended to complement the *Things to do* associated with Labels and Stereotypes].

3 Divide pupils into groups of four or five. Each group is a television production team. They are to make to make a documentary film called 'Colour Doesn't Matter'. The purpose of the film is to show that people of all colours have achieved, and continue to achieve, great things, and that the most sensible and effective way forward will be for people of all nations to work together in racial harmony.

The task for the groups is to decide:
- what examples they might include of different nations and races working together, or playing together (e.g. the Olympic Games);
- who they might wish to interview;
- whether they might wish to include film from past history;
- what scenes they might create of an imaginary future in which people of different nations and colours are working happily together.

4 Construct a whole class/group collage comprising a wide range of examples of racial harmony, using pictures and images cut from magazines or colour supplements. Ask pupils to suggest a suitable title.

5 Divide pupils into small groups. Ask them to discuss the situation outlined in the passage *For reflection* i.e. 'What if you were your mother or father whose child (you) arrived home very, very late after playing with friends?'

How would you feel? What courses of action would you consider?

What would you do? How would you deal with your child when he or she arrived home?

As the child, what action would you expect your parent(s) to take?

In a whole class/group sharing session, compare points that have been raised during discussions in the groups.

See also

The Amazing World of Mankind

Curiosity

Them and Us

Points of View

Labels and Stereotypes

THEM AND US

Focus

To consider who are THEM and US;

To explore the similarities as well as the differences between THEM and US.

For reflection

Them and us: us and them.

What do we mean when we use these two words? Who are we referring to?

US usually means me and those with whom I have something in common:
- me and my family – we all belong to the same family group;
- me and my group of friends;
- me and all the other boys and girls in our team, in our class, or in our school;
- me and all those who support the same team;
- me and all those who belong to my country and speak the same language;
- me and all those who agree with me!

Can you think of other examples?

THEM means people who are different from me in some way. For example:
- maybe they have a different group of friends;
- or they attend a different school;
- or they support a different team;
- or they speak a different language;
- or they don't agree with what I think or what I say!

Can you add to this list?

Often, there seems to be almost a sense of competition between us and them. *Us* seems to suggest 'we are right', while *them* suggests 'they must be wrong because they are different from us'. In other words 'we are better than them'.

But remember, *we are all both us and them!* For example, we might refer to the people of another country as 'them', while the people of that country refer to 'us' as 'them'. So, we are both 'us' and them' – and whatever we are called, 'us' or 'them', we are still the same people with the same intelligence, the same feelings and, of course, the same good looks! We don't suddenly change into monsters because someone else thinks of us as 'them'.

We also use *them* when we are saying something that is not particularly kind or complimentary about other people. For example, we use 'them' when we speak of people who perform unpopular duties. Traffic wardens are an obvious example. Can you think of others?

Them is also used when we are referring to groups of people who make decisions that affect our lives everyday – groups such as the government, the local council, those responsible for the running of hospitals, and so on. (Can you name other similar groups we often blame when things go wrong, or when we can't have what we want?)

We blame 'them'!
- There's a hole in the road that hasn't been repaired – it's the council's fault (them);
- 'I had to queue twenty minutes to buy a stamp today. They ('the Post Office' – 'them') should put more staff on!'

Often, of course, we don't know the people we are blaming. We've probably not met them nor seen them, and might not even know their names, but we are prepared to blame 'them'.

But just as *we* don't change when someone from another country thinks of us as *them*, the same is true of others. You may have a best friend who supports a different soccer team, likes different music from you and has a different coloured skin. In all of these ways your friend might be described as belonging to *them*, – but because he is a really nice person – despite these differences - you get on well and are good pals.

In a similar way, the stranger sitting next to you in the cinema, who laughs at the same things as you and is obviously a fun person to be with, might well be a traffic warden! It is *the task* the warden performs that is unpopular, not the traffic warden as a person. And, of course, the same could be true of the councillors and all the other people we blame and refer to as *them*.

Perhaps next time we use the word *them*, and especially if we want to be critical, we shall remember that there is a difference between someone as a person and the duties they have to perform as part of their job. *Them* and *us* are *mask words* and, like masks, they hide what the people behind the masks are really like. What is in front of the mask is just 'show'. It is what is behind the mask that matters.

Things to do

1 Ask pupils to collect photographs – from newspapers, colour supplements and magazines – to illustrate the *Them* and *Us* theme. It would be helpful to have examples showing divisions and differences between groups, and examples in which people with contrasting or conflicting interests successfully live, work and play together (for example, rich and poor, football supporters, mixed races).

   Use the images as stimuli for pupil comment and discussion – perhaps asking pupils, working in small groups, to provide captions and/or commentary.

2 The purpose of this activity is to demonstrate that THEM and US groups often form in a very arbitrary way – by accident rather than by design. And yet, once formed, they can become closed and divisive.

   Provide each pupil with a sheet of paper. At the centre of each, the pupil should write the word 'ME', perhaps enclosed in a circle or rectangle. The pupil should then surround 'ME' with the names of different 'US' groups of which he or she is a part. Several examples are included in the *For reflection* passage, but it is important for each pupil to make an individual and personal selection. Most pupils will have little difficulty in identifying seven or eight groups. A few will double that number.

   When this stage is completed, ask pupils to consider *why* and *how they came to belong* to each particular group. For example:

   - It is likely that the pupil belongs to some of the groups listed by accident rather than by choice, e.g. we don't choose the family we are born into, nor our nationality, nor the language we speak – and often, as children, we have little choice regarding which school we attend. A letter 'A' (for 'accident') should be placed against any group to which the pupil belongs by accident rather than choice.

   - Some groups will comprise pupils with similar interests, e.g. those who attend the same extra-curricular clubs, or support the same football team . A letter 'I' (for 'interest') should be placed against these groups.

- Some groups will bring together pupils with particular skills, e.g. sports teams, musicians receiving instrumental lessons. A letter 'S' (for 'skill') should be placed against these groups.

- Friendship groups sometimes change from one activity to another, but if the group is fairly constant it should be marked with a letter 'F' (for 'friendship').

Pupils may have other reasons. If so, what are they?

3 In this activity pupils can directly experience the feeling of being both US and THEM according to different criteria selected by you.

To begin the activity pupils should be seated. When you define a particular group, pupils to whom that description applies should stand, forming an US group. The pupils who remain seated are THEM. For example, the description might be, 'Those who sing in the school choir'.

Those pupils stand (or move to a specified area in the room), and sufficient time is allowed to mentally note the composition of the group.

When a second description is given – say, 'Those who have represented the school in some sporting activity' – it is likely that some of those standing will sit, and some of those sitting will stand. The changed composition of the US and THEM groups will be commented on before a third description is announced. And so the activity continues for as long as is appropriate.

The choice of descriptors can best be decided by you, to fit in with the ethos of the school and local circumstances. It is important that opportunities are provided for all pupils to participate.

The activity should be concluded with a brief discussion of any differences pupils experienced between being one of US and being one of THEM.

4 Working in small groups, ask pupils to make a list of situations in which people like to blame THEM – 'others', officials, those in charge – rather than accept responsibility themselves. For example, a traffic warden cannot issue a parking ticket unless a driver is breaking the law. It is the driver's responsibility not to break the law.

Can pupils think of instances when they themselves might unfairly blame others – including situations in the home, at school, or on the sports field?

See also

Points of View

Labels and Stereotypes

Caring For and Caring About

Freedom

I Wish

POINTS OF VIEW

Focus

To encourage pupils to respect the views and opinions of others, even though they might not agree with them.

For reflection

One day a race took place between a hare and a fox in an attempt to settle an argument about who was the faster runner. On this occasion the hare was the winner. The result of the race was reported in the following morning's newspapers. In huge letters, the headlines in the *Hare Times* read 'HARE FIRST! FOX LAST!' while equally bold headlines in the *Fox Telegraph* announced 'FOX SECOND! HARE LAST BUT ONE!'

Of course, both statements were right, but they told only part of the story. The papers had failed to mention that there were only two competitors in the race. The reporters had chosen to see things from a *particular point of view*, and had given their readers a very one-sided account of what had actually taken place.

In fact, most of us do similar things every day – we select the information that suits us and choose to see what we want to see.

For example, if we like someone we tend to look only at their good points. We agree mostly with what they have to say, and we find excuses for any weaknesses they may have. On the other hand, if we dislike someone we tend to look for their faults. We question what they say, and may not notice their good points.

Someone once said it is like looking at something through pieces of coloured glass. What you see has a different appearance according to the colour chosen, and all are quite different from what you see if you look through plain glass.

When people hold different opinions from each other, we say they have *different points of view*, and that is a very helpful way of describing what actually happens. Imagine a circle of pupils, with one person in the middle. If that person stands perfectly still, (as if frozen, like a statue) but everyone in the circle moves four paces to their right and then stops, each pupil's view of the person in the middle will be changed from where they first started. Maybe the first view was a side view with the person facing left. Four paces to the right is likely to provide a back view. And so one could continue, to have a different side-view, and then a front view – not to mention all of the different views in between. And yet the person in the centre hasn't changed – it is the point of view that has changed.

Parents and children often have different points of view.

Imagine, for example, that just as you are about to leave for school, it starts to rain. It is only light rain, but the sky is cloudy. Your mother thinks you should take a raincoat, but you don't want to.

What reasons do you think your mother would use to support her point of view? What arguments might you use?

Or imagine a different situation:

You would like a puppy for your birthday but your parents are not keen on the idea. Can you imagine the different points of view?

Do you think that by the time you are a parent your point of view will be different from what it is now? Why?

Every day there are occasions when we have to decide what we think, or how we feel, about a whole range of things – and often we're not slow in telling others what we think! In fact, we live in an age when we are encouraged to express views. Advertisements for radio and television phone-in programmes tell us, 'We want to hear your views. We want to hear what you think. So why not give us a ring on 0800 000 000!'

The poem you are going to hear shows that when we express a point of view we believe is right, it is possible that other people may have a different point of view that is equally 'right'.

The poem is called 'The Blind Man and the Elephant'

The Blind Man and the Elephant

It was six men of Indostan,
To learning much inclined,
Who went to see the elephant
(Though all of them were blind),
That each by observation
Might satisfy his mind.

The first approached the elephant,
And happening to fall
Against his broad and sturdy side,
At once began to bawl,
'God bless me! but the elephant
Is very like a wall!'

The second, feeling of the tusk,
Cried – 'Ho! what have we here
So very round and smooth and sharp?
To me it's mighty clear,
This wonder of an elephant
Is very like a spear!'

The third approached the animal
And happening to take
The squirming trunk within his hands
Thus boldly up and spake:
'I see' – quoth he – 'the elephant
Is very like a snake!'

The fourth reached out his eager hand,
And felt about the knee;
'What most this wondrous beast is like
Is mighty pain – quoth he –
'It's clear enough the elephant
Is very like a tree!'

The fifth, who chanced to touch the ear,
Said – 'Even the blindest man
Can tell what this resembles most;
Deny the fact who can,
This marvel of an elephant
Is very like a fan!'

The sixth no sooner had begun
About the beast to grope,
Than, seizing on the swinging tail
That fell within his scope,
'I see' – quoth he – 'the elephant
Is very like a rope!'

> And so these men of Indostan
> Disputed loud and long,
> Each in his own opinion
> Exceeding stiff and strong,
> Though each was partly in the right,
> And all were in the wrong!
>
> *John G Saxe*

It is important that we should respect the opinions of others, even if we don't agree with them. We must realise that *we are not always right*. We are only offering *our point of view*.

Things to do

1 To reinforce the concept of 'points of view', arrange small groups of pupils in circles, as for an observational drawing lesson, and provide each pupil with drawing materials. Ask pupils to divide their paper into four. Place before each group a suitable still-life object – such as a mug/tankard, a shoe, a school bag, an angle-poise lamp etc – and, in one quarter of their paper, ask pupils to draw the object as it appears to them. After a short while (decide when based on the speed of progress) rotate the object through 90 degrees and, using a second square on their paper, ask pupils to draw the object as they now see it. Repeat the process twice more, so that the pupils finish with an object drawn from four points of view.

What is different about each angle?

What new information does each view provide?

2 Provide pupils with reports from three or four newspapers covering the same news item. Include a mixture of tabloid and broadsheet reports. Working in small groups, ask pupils to compare the reports, commenting on:
- *the headlines*
  How are they trying to attract attention? Are they sensational? Do they attempt to shock or rouse emotions? Are they amusing? Do they summarise appropriately what the report or article is about? Who are the headlines trying to attract – what sort of readers?
- *the factual detail*
  Do all of the reports contain exactly the same facts? Do they agree?

Are any facts left out in some reports, or others added?
- *the slant of the report*
  Are the facts reported in an emotional way – that is, is the reporter trying to persuade the reader to a particular point of view?
  Do pupils feel that the reports are honest and can be trusted?

3 Working either in small groups or in pairs, ask pupils to prepare dialogue for, and perform, a scene of parent and child conflict. Pupils should be allowed to choose their own theme if they wish. Alternatively, they could use on of the two outlined in the *For reflection* passage, or one of the following:
   Wanting to stay up to watch a horror movie
   Wanting to buy unsuitable clothes
   Disagreement about the choice of friends
   Condition of their bedroom
   Pocket money.

   The whole class should be involved in the discussion of issues arising from the performances, but the focus should be on *recognising and respecting different points of view*.

4 Ask pupils to keep a personal diary for one or two days in which they make a brief note of situations in which their view has been different from someone else's. Ask them to asterisk any occasions when more than two people each expressed a different view.

   Looking back over the various instances recorded:
   - Did the pupil learn anything from others' points of view?
   - Did anything that was said change or influence the pupil's own thinking?
   - Has the pupil since thought of things he or she wishes they had said but didn't say?

5 Ask pupils to discuss, 'Are there occasions when it might be more sensible *not* to express a point of view?' If they think 'yes' can they give examples?

See also

Them and Us

Thinking

There's No-one Quite Like You